KU-387-622

MAHLER'S SIXTH SYMPHONY – A STUDY

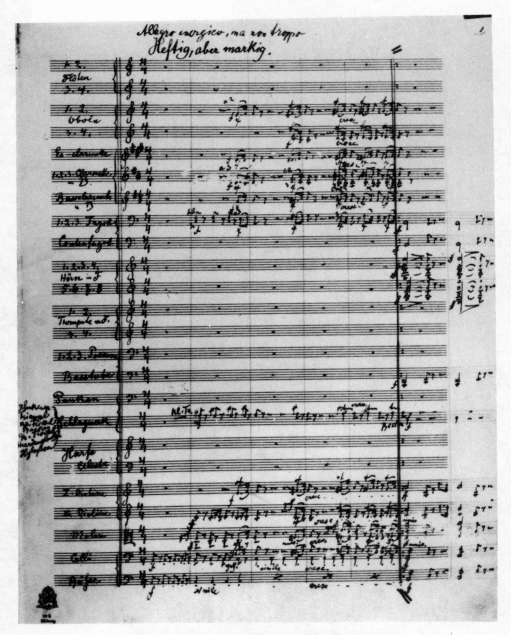

Autograph first page of Mahler's Sixth Symphony

MAHLER'S SIXTH
SYMPHONY
—*A Study*

Norman Del Mar

with an Introduction by
Colin Matthews

EULENBURG BOOKS

LONDON

Ernst Eulenburg Ltd
48 Great Marlborough Street
London W1V 1DB

Copyright © 1980 Norman Del Mar

ISBN 0 903873 29 X

Printed and bound in Great Britain by
REDWOOD BURN LIMITED
Trowbridge and Esher

Condition of sale: This book is sold subject to the condition that it shall not, by way
of trade or otherwise, be lent, re-sold, hired out or otherwise circulated without the
Publisher's prior consent, in any form of binding or cover other than that in which it
is published and without a similar condition including this condition being imposed
on the subsequent purchaser.

For Donald Mitchell
in admiration and gratitude

Contents

Illustrations

Introduction

'The only Sixth, despite the Pastoral'. It would be amusing to know how many readers of Alban Berg's assessment have reacted indulgently or indignantly to his perhaps deliberate hyperbole. Especially since – as Norman Del Mar makes clear to us in his opening chapter – very few of those readers, in Britain or the United States at least, could have had the opportunity to hear the Sixth Symphony for a good fifty years after it was composed. Now we have a whole book devoted to it, and performances are frequent. So with our ability to make a confident judgement of the work, what should we make of Berg's remark?

Perhaps we should consider first how well do we know the symphony. Its title 'The Tragic', although not, so far as we know, Mahler's own, is a particularly apt one; but Norman Del Mar is right to point out that Mahler's motivation for writing a tragic symphony in 1903 is far from clear. He was than at the height of his fame as a conductor; beginning to have real success as a composer; and, at the relatively late age of forty, at last enjoying a settled life with a wife and children.

Alma Mahler herself testifies to Mahler's happiness and confidence at that time: 'he was serene; he was conscious of the greatness of his work'. If it were not for the fact that Mahler's extraordinary creativity was continuously renewed and refreshed each summer that he spent composing, one might say that the years 1903 and 1904 showed him at the height of his powers. In 1903 he composed the first three movements of the Sixth Symphony; in 1904 not only did he compose the great finale, but the last two of the *Kindertotenlieder* and the two *Nachtmusik* 'serenades' of the Seventh Symphony as well. (His younger daughter Anna was born in the midst of all this creativity!)

It would, of course, be foolish to assume that a happy man will of necessity write happy music. In a famous letter to Nadezhda von Meck, Tchaikovsky wrote that 'without any special reason for rejoicing, I may be moved by the most cheerful creative mood, and vice versa, a work composed in the happiest surroundings may be touched with dark and gloomy colours'. This is surely likely to be true of any composer. The Sixth Symphony is, at the objective level, perfectly comprehensible: there is no need to speculate about Mahler foretelling his own future in the finale, with its 'three blows of fate'.

But that particular movement is not just 'touched with dark and gloomy colours'. Within its half-hour span it embraces every subjective emotion – through fear, anxiety, defiance, and the extremes of exhilaration and exuberance, before sinking to the depths of despair. In that sense it is truly tragic: unlike, say, the last movement of Tchaikovsky's

Sixth Symphony, it is not self-evident that the work will end unhappily. In his analysis of the finale Norman Del Mar writes of the moment before the catastrophic collapse: 'the drama seems at an end, the hero has surely triumphed.' It is, of course, impossible to draw back from our knowledge of the work and pretend that we do not know what will happen; but it is undeniable that, for all its ultimate defeat, there is more exultancy in the Sixth Symphony's finale than in any other of Mahler's works.

This ambivalence is what gives the music its special power. The defeat is noble and heroic; there is no equivocation about it, but at the same time a total absence of self pity. For all Mahler's self-involvement and identification with the symphony it is, notwithstanding, his most objective work – one might almost say his most impersonal, since the extraordinary power of the music transcends the purely personal to become universal.

For the listener, the absolute tragedy of the symphony is, ultimately, cathartic. But for Mahler this could not be so. The symphony's personal meaning grew deeper and more disturbing to him. Though we should not forget that the year of its first performance – 1906 – was also the year of the creation of the Eighth Symphony, it was at the very same time that, out of superstitious fear, he removed the third and fatal hammer blow from the score.

Could the confusion about the order of the middle movements possibly derive from the same fear of the symphony's power? Norman Del Mar is undoubtedly correct in maintaining that the Andante must precede the Scherzo. But the vague tradition that Mahler had changed his mind (a tradition so vague that Erwin Ratz's decision to tamper with the order has no documentary evidence at all to support it) *might* derive from a desire on Mahler's part to weaken the symphony further. But whatever the cause of the confusion, there is no *musical* case for playing the Scherzo before the Andante, any more than there is a case for omitting the third hammer blow in performance. We should be aware of Mahler's indecision, but – as Norman Del Mar points out – we no longer need fear for his life.

How well, then, do we know this symphony? Not so well as yet to be able to unravel all of its enigmas. Certainly not so well as Norman Del Mar. But well enough to agree with Berg that this is a remarkable and exceptional work. No need to make invidious comparisons with the only Sixth Symphony that can rival it – that was not Berg's intention. One need only consider how few individual symphonies there are (and not just sixth symphonies) that do not merely deserve, but virtually demand a full-scale study: that is the measure of the work's greatness.

To those who know and love Mahler, the Sixth Symphony occupies a special place. The works that precede it are perhaps more direct and lovable; those that follow it more immediately moving and comprehensible (although the Seventh Symphony to some extent shares the objectivity of its predecessor). The Sixth is granite-like and unyielding, yet its superb construction conceals – or perhaps rather reveals – Mahler's humanity as does no other of his symphonies. In adopting for the first and only time the conventional classical scheme, Mahler both affirmed his mastery of symphonic form and showed that its constraints only stimulated him to greater invention.

It is all too easy for his admirers to take for granted Mahler's mastery, or for his critics to ignore it. Norman Del Mar's penetrating and exhaustive study will compel both to return to the music with renewed insight and excitement. It is a tribute not only to his own love and understanding of Mahler, but also to the composer who can inspire such a response.

Colin Matthews

Chapter One

The Genesis and Significance of the Symphony

Mahler began to sketch the Sixth Symphony at his beautiful lakeside retreat at Maiernigg during the early summer of 1903. He was forty-three years old and at the height of his career and fame, in the middle of his reign as autocratic director of the Vienna Court Opera – a reign that lasted no less than ten years, from 1897 to 1907.

Few men can have made more enemies or have been more feared than this eternally uncompromising dictator, this complex introvert, self-centred almost to the point of paranoia, and a fanatical seeker after the highest artistic standards – in himself no less than in others. A twisted personality, grotesquely idiosyncratic, his conducting career had sprung rapidly from his stormy studentship, forcing him by the nature of this arduous professional activity into the straitjacket of a regular life-pattern, both as interpreter and composer.

Nevertheless, if he was feared and even hated he was also deeply admired, as is borne out not only by the comments of his contemporaries, artists and critics alike, but especially by his succession of appointments as conductor in artistic centres each larger, more prestigious and demanding than the last. After two short periods during which he held positions in obscure localities the ascent is breath-taking: Cassel, Leipzig, Budapest, Hamburg, Vienna. Psychologically, the cost must have been severe, and above all to a martinet and perfectionist such as Mahler, whose heart moreover was resolutely set on further self-expression through composition.

The parallel with the early career of Richard Strauss might seem obvious but there was a strong difference that lay in the innate abilities as well as the utterly opposed characters of the two men. Strauss was a born natural composer, but *au fond* an easy-going humourous fellow to whom the highly desirable conducting positions which fell so effort-lessly into his lap (Meiningen, Munich, Berlin) formed an agreeable professional background to his main preoccupation in life – composition. Mahler was a born conductor, constitutionally unable to give anything less than the whole of himself throughout his periods of duty as musical director, whether at Laibach (better known now as Ljubljana) or Budapest – let alone Vienna. The ceaseless naggings of his genius, that vein of fantastical creativity that he so ruthlessly suppressed during his seasons of operatic and concert work, burst out only at his annual holiday-times, turning these into periods of perhaps even greater mental exhaustion.

And from early years, after surprisingly few tentative steps in other directions, Mahler fell into the way of converting these spasmodic creative outbursts into symphonies, each embodying in its sprawling, utterly unconventional length and layout all the multifarious things that had been building up within him, waiting for the moment and the vehicle for their release. Yet unlike Strauss, Mahler had to work desperately hard to find the right medium for this expression both in style and form. Although it might seem now that he must have known from the beginning that he would write a First Symphony and then follow it up with Nos. 2 and 3, and so on for the rest of his life, in fact the starting point for so regular a symphonic output, as it turned out to be, was by no means a matter of positive creative policy.

The First Symphony, as we know it, began life as a so-called 'Symphonic Poem' in five movements divided into two parts, the successor to the startlingly original cantata-symphony *Das klagende Lied*. Completed in its first three-part version as far back as 1880 when Mahler was only twenty, this might almost have seemed suitable material for an opera, especially bearing in mind Mahler's natural feeling for vocal composition. The list of early works contains many songs and sketches for operas never completed. This greatest of all operatic conductors never completed a single original stage-work of his own,[1] following instead a destiny that turned him into a composer exclusively of songs and symphonies. For Mahler soon decided to revise and curtail his symphonic poem, which had been performed on 27 October 1893 under the title of 'Titan' with graphic programme titles for each of the five movements, the new work in only four movements being described purely and simply as 'Symphony No. 1 in D major'.

At once the pattern of his life work was set for the future. A huge funeral-march epilogue revealed itself clearly as a first movement for a second symphony, the remainder of the monumental structure we recognize today as the *Resurrection* Symphony only forming its superb architecture gradually, and indeed piecemeal, in the mind of its creator. Thus the introduction of voices into the new symphony through the inclusion of an actual *Knaben Wunderhorn* song followed by a full-scale choral apotheosis, was by no means part of a preconceived plan when Mahler drafted the great first movement which is so clearly linked with the programmatic finale. But even when the work had so vastly out-

---

[1] This is not to ignore Mahler's completion of Weber's *Die drei Pintos* which, although it contains much original composition by Mahler, cannot stand to his credit as an independent stage-work.

grown its basic symphonic format Mahler still did not hesitate to entitle it 'Symphony No. 2 in C minor'. And thereafter, each of the new works to be composed summer by summer in his rest periods (as they should have been) came to be designated as another numbered symphony, apart, that is, from the Lieder which lie behind so many of them. It is a strange phenomenon that Mahler should have seen himself already committed to such a sequence of works regardless of shape, or of the forces required for performance, or even resemblance to the traditional scheme of the symphony as he had inherited it. In this his nearest precedents were of course the equally untraditional, all-embracing symphony-effusions of that other composer-conductor, Hector Berlioz, as exemplified not only by the *Symphonie fantastique* but by the so-called 'Symphonie dramatique' *Roméo et Juliette*.

Thus, by the time Mahler had reached what must surely have been the summit of his ambitions as a conductor, the Vienna Opera, he had three of these mammoth symphonies to his credit, for no sooner was the C minor Symphony complete than another followed hard on its heels, longer and even more complex than its predecessors. In fact a case could be made for regarding Mahler's Third Symphony as the most elaborately conceived of all his works, the one most nearly fulfilling his famous dictum when arguing with Sibelius that 'the symphony must encompass the world'. Indeed, even Mahler must have recognised that he was over-filling his canvas when at the eleventh hour he docked his scheme of its final portion to be kept in reserve for a fourth symphony, even though 'Das himmlisches Leben', the *Knaben Wunderhorn* setting of which it consisted, was thematically linked with more than one of the earlier movements of the Third Symphony for which it had been originally planned to stand as finale.

During almost the whole of the crucial ten-year period that was to follow, Mahler spent his summer holidays at that summer-house in Carinthia called Schwarzenfels on the shores of the Wörthersee, near the village of Maiernigg; and there in due succession the Fourth Symphony followed the Third, and the Fifth came shortly after, Mahler continuing to spend his compositional vacations there after his marriage in March 1902 to the beautiful and fascinating Alma Maria Schindler, with whom he had been violently in love ever since their first meeting five months earlier. Already the following November their elder daughter was born, Maria Ann, who was to die so tragically in childhood during 1907 – a fateful year for Mahler in which he was to learn of the heart-condition that would soon cause his own death.

But in 1903 when he set to work on the sixth of his series of symphonies, the 'Tragic' as it is often called although not by Mahler himself, there seemed hardly a cloud on the horizon of his fortunes.

There is a paradox here that is hard to understand, especially as this was to be the most personal, the most directly self-involved, of all his symphonies. Alma recalled that at the time of its composition Mahler 'was serene; he was conscious of the greatness of his work. He was a tree in full leaf and flower'. Moreover he was obviously enjoying the partially 'Symphonia Domestica' side of the work. Mahler himself proclaimed, for instance, that the second subject of the opening movement was specifically intended as a portrait of his adored Almschi. And it required no very great stretch of the imagination to see the stormy but heroic material of the primary subject-matter as a self-character-study.

Yet the Symphony's key of A minor is not without its own significance, nor the fact that the work begins and ends in that same key, most of Mahler's symphonies having a progressive system of tonalities over the span of the movements. Donald Mitchell points with justifiable emphasis[2] to the particularly tragic quality this key had for Mahler, representing 'either chilling, felling strokes of fate' – as in the symphony under consideration – 'or a kind of desperate passion' – as in the second movement of the Fifth, the Rondo Burleske of the Ninth, and, above all the opening 'Drinking Song of the Misery of the Earth' from *Das Lied von der Erde*. Mitchell also points out that the catastrophic close of *Das klagende Lied* is in A minor and that the key must have already had a strong power of association in the young Mahler's creative consciousness for there is believed to have been an early symphony of 1880-2 (since disappeared) in that key as well as a still earlier Piano Quartet in A minor.

Even so, there is little in the first three movements to warrant the widely-accepted 'Tragic' title of the symphony. For all its ferocious energy and dramatic 'catastrophes', the opening Allegro ends exultantly. The Scherzo which originally came second in the order of the movements undoubtedly possesses a generous share of Mahler's favourite demonic savagery, especially in the way it distorts elements of the first movement in the Mephistophelian manner of Liszt's *Faust* Symphony. This, however, was a typical stylistic trademark scarcely justifying the search for some extra-musical programmatic significance. Least of all, needless to say, does the E flat major Andante strike a note of tragedy in the true sense of the term, for all the heart-rending nostalgia of its closing pages.

Here lies escape from reality, and its distant tonal centre mirrors that of the A flat intermezzo-like Andante of the C minor Second Symphony.

We know that by the end of the summer vacation of 1903 at least the first two movements were fully sketched, whereas the finale was only

[2] *Gustav Mahler: The Early Years*, Rockliff, London, 1958, p.134.

worked out the following summer. And it is essentially this enormous structure, representing nearly half of the whole span of the symphony, with its hammer-blows of fate, its closing débâcle and dirge, and its pessimistic view of the composer himself as the heroic victim of malignant forces ranged against him 'to fell him as a tree' in the famous phrase quoted by his wife, that earns the work its 'Tragic' connotation.

This might lead one to expect some changes in Mahler's fortunes at this time, but on the contrary three more years were to pass before fate did in fact strike. It seems rather that, ever superstitiously aware of a constantly threatening destiny lying in wait for him – like Thurber's 'claw of the sea-puss' from *My Life and Hard Times* which, we are assured, 'gets us all in the end'; or like Henry James's 'beast in the jungle' which similarly lurks in wait for each of us, Mahler allowed himself to become over-involved emotionally in some personal application of the symphony, believing it to contain a prophetic message relevant to his own life and future. We read in Alma's Memoirs[3] of the appalling effect the finale had upon him, so much so that 'out of shame and anxiety he did not conduct the symphony well. He hesitated to bring out the dark omen behind this terrible last movement.'

Yet, although Alma's 'dark omen' may well be somewhat naively prophetic, at the same time it is hard to account for this truly tragic finale. Since, however, there is generally a strong emotional and philosophical link between Mahler's symphonies and the songs of the same period, guidance might reasonably be found in the *Kindertotenlieder* whose echoes are indeed to be found in some of the organic material of the Sixth Symphony's finale, as Mitchell has shown.[4] These poignantly tragic songs, though begun already in 1901, were not completed until the summer of 1904 when two further songs (the third and fourth) were added to the three of the original inspiration. Thus, together with the other Rückert songs, published as part of the *Sieben letzte Lieder*, they bridge the periods of the Fifth and Sixth symphonies and were completed at the same time as the finale of the Sixth with which significantly they share more than one thematic idea.

Theodore Reik, a Viennese-born disciple of Freud, and himself a psychoanalyst, published in New York in 1953 a book entitled *The Haunting Melody* in which he presented a contentious view of Mahler and his work but one which has at least to be taken into account in seeking the answer to the many problems surrounding this extraordinary man. In the course of his thesis Reik puts forward the case

[3] *Gustav Mahler, Memories and Letters*, ed. Donald Mitchell, London, 1946; further enlarged edition, 1973.

[4] Donald Mitchell: *Gustav Mahler: The Wunderhorn Years*, London, 1976, pp.40-42.

that Mahler's choice of the Rückert poems was based not on prophetic insight but on the memory of his own dead infant brother Ernst. However much justification Reik may well have had for this conjecture, there is no doubt that Alma was intensely affected with superstitious dread and this in turn may well have reflected on the composer's own state of mind. 'To my mind', Alma wrote in her autobiography,[5] 'there was something eerie about it: in the garden these two wonderfully gifted children were squealing with joy, and in his study Mahler could sing of their death . . .' It is certainly curious that hereafter there follows a complete gap in Mahler's Lieder output, until the hybrid songs of *Das Lied von der Erde* of 1908. However, if one accepts Mahler's own assessment of the Bethge settings primarily as movements of a symphony rather than a group of orchestral Lieder, the Rückert songs of which the *Kindertotenlieder* form the climax become his last in the genre, a remarkable fact in a composer whose entire output can be said to germinate from the Lied.

For a link of superstition can be traced between precisely these three works – the Sixth Symphony; the *Kindertotenlieder*; *Das Lied von der Erde* – and the threefold catastrophe that afflicted Mahler in 1907: his downfall in Vienna; the death of his own elder daughter; the pronouncement of his own fatal heart-disease. In the finale of the Symphony Mahler really believed that he had predicted his three blows at the hands of a savage destiny; in the songs he seemed to have foretold the loss of his darling little Putzi; and when he came to write the Song-Symphony, two years after fate had actually struck, he had a further premonition that stopped him from designating it as 'No.9' which properly it should have been. The precedent of Beethoven and Bruckner held him back, even though he decided to subtitle it 'Eine Symphonie'. Of course in the event fate ironically rebounded upon him, since he really did die after completing a symphony which he steeled himself to call by the dreaded number, at the same time hastily drafting a Tenth – which he failed to complete. But it is *Das Lied*, the first work he wrote after the shattering diagnosis, that in reality is the fateful Ninth, and ends with his own heart-breaking farewell to life and song, to his 'liebe Erde'.

Furthermore, once this superstition took hold of Mahler's mind it inevitably affected his creativity, which became less purposeful and even less assured. The Seventh Symphony, for all its remarkable central movements, is generally accepted as being the least successful of the series. However much one is intrigued by Mahler's virtuosity and the passionate involvement of his assertive style, the truth cannot be evaded that the outer movements, and the finale in particular, lack the

[5] *And the Bridge is Love*, Hutchinson, London, 1958.

spontaneity – the inevitability – that always characterize Mahler's greatest creations. Even the monumental Eighth Symphony is not without its weaknesses that emerge when it is placed in the context of Mahler's output as a whole and viewed with critical detachment instead of the wonder with which one understandably finds oneself regarding this mightiest of symphonies. For the very text 'Veni, Creator Spiritus' seems to have come into Mahler's mind with singular aptness in his particular psychological circumstances, these being perhaps the springboard for its choice. Alma wrote in her Memoirs of the year 1906:

> After we arrived at Maiernigg, there was the usual fortnight during which, nearly every year, he was haunted by the spectre of failing inspiration. Then one morning, just as he crossed the threshold of his studio up in the wood, it came to him – 'Veni, Creator Spiritus'. He composed and wrote down the whole opening chorus to the half-forgotten words. . . .

Alma's 'nearly every year' is hardly consistent with her own accounts of the preceding years. There had surely been no spectre of sterility in the long and concentrated period of combined song and symphonic composition that culminated in the Sixth Symphony. But thereafter it was quite a different matter.

In later life Richard Strauss acknowledged that he found dependence on words a vital prop for failing musical invention. This may indeed have been temporarily true also of Mahler during this quasi-hiatus in his creative initiative. Undoubtedly the choice of the texts for the Eighth Symphony and the adoption of a symphonic form more unconventional than any since the Third Symphony – it was incidentally the first completely choral symphony ever written – could be considered a stroke of genius in itself. But the execution of the fantastic scheme with its alliance of the Latin hymn to the mystical closing scene from the second part of Goethe's *Faust* is not flawless. Michael Kennedy[6] courageously detects a stylistic throwback in the first movement and *longueurs* betraying flagging inspiration in the second. It is indeed not hard to agree that, for all the pioneering quality of the concept, much of the music itself is the least forward-looking of all Mahler's later output. It was actually written in an unusually short space of time during this 'last summer of peace and beauty and content' as Alma called it. Mahler told Schönberg that he had felt as if it had been dictated to him (an experience shared by other composers such as Elgar and Rachmaninov), and he subjected the draft to exceptionally little revision. This seems by definition to postulate an indisputable aesthetic value, whereas the true value of the Eighth as a transitional work only ultimately comes into

[6] *Mahler:* in 'The Master Musicians' series. Dent, London, 1974.

focus when set alongside the supreme achievements that followed it.

In 1907, as already described, fate really did strike Mahler and with three truly crushing blows. Firstly it was this summer during which Marie, his and Alma's eldest daughter, their little Putzi, contracted scarlet fever and diphtheria and died on 5 July; it was during 1907 also that social pressures in Vienna, together with crises at the opera-house itself, reached their climax – to the point where Mahler saw no option but to relinquish the power he had wielded so ruthlessly but to such artistic purpose for the last ten years, his resignation taking effect in August although his last performance (*Fidelio*) was actually given in October; and finally between January and the summer of 1907 a series of consultations with a succession of specialists revealed the serious nature of Mahler's own health, his heart-condition being finally diagnosed in terms that amounted to nothing short of a death-sentence.

Then at last he sensed that he had indeed been 'felled like a tree', and perversely enough only then, with superstitious dread replaced by tragic actuality, inspiration returned to him in full measure, enabling him to produce in his last year two masterpieces of the highest rank, the symphonic song-cycle *Das Lied von der Erde* and its companion work, the Ninth Symphony.

When therefore, with Mahler's whole achievement spread before us, the final pattern is made clear, it is possible to see that the Sixth Symphony occupies a central position, marking as it does a turning point not only in his work but in his life as well, inseparable as they can be shown to be. The progress from tragedy to optimism, so striking a feature of the Fifth Symphony, is diametrically reversed in the Sixth, and in this, apart from its intrinsic quality and stature, its unique inner cohesion and the strength, power and inevitability of its thematic material, lies its unassailable importance in the broad view of its creator's work. It is thus the more remarkable that this has been so belatedly reflected in concert-programmes, even though Mahler's successors such as Schönberg and Webern had long since recognized both the merits and importance of its innovatory features, many of which they incorporated into their own works.

The neglect into which the Sixth Symphony had fallen is shown by the fact that its first American performance seems to have been as late as December 1947 when it was given in New York by Mitropoulos. I am myself credited by Michael Kennedy as having been the first to present it in this country in my broadcast performance with the BBC Symphony Orchestra in October 1956 but, gratifying as this may be, I believe that a performance was in fact given some twenty years earlier with the same orchestra, which was to have been conducted by none other than Anton Webern himself but was ultimately taken over by

Sir Adrian Boult. (A highly entertaining photograph of Webern re-hearsing the symphony is reproduced in Marc Vignal's splendidly-illustrated study of Mahler in the 'Solfèges' series.)[7]

In any case, even the late 1930s constitutes a sufficient delay in the propagation of so important a work – over thirty years after its com-position and twenty-five after the death of its author. Not even the comparative neglect of Mahler's work as a whole can fully account for it. It can hardly be doubted that at least some blame can be attributed to the circumstances of its publication and the different versions presented by the various editions of the score even when it did once again become available after a long period during which it was the hardest to acquire of all the Mahler scores. It is part of the purpose of the present volume to explore and compare these versions in some detail, and this study – after an intermediary chapter concerned with a com-prehensive analysis of the symphony – will form the basis of the substantial third chapter together with, it is hoped, evidence enough to support the claim that this work represents a central and crucial pillar in the output of one who, so far from being no more than a secondary composer of eccentric Kapellmeistermusik, as so many critics and colleagues believed – 'no composer at all, just a very great conductor', Richard Strauss once misguidedly said – was in fact one of the greatest symphonists who ever lived.

---

[7] Editions du Seuil, Paris, 1966.

Chapter Two

Part 1: Thematic Analysis

I

EXPOSITION
(beginning—**14**)

1st subject (beginning—**6**+4) Tonal centre A minor

(cf. Liszt Piano Concerto in E♭)

(cf. Schumann *Manfred* Overture)

Motto (Fate motifs) A major/minor

Transition (**7**—**8**) Tonal centre remains A minor

(Chorale)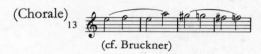

(cf. Bruckner)

2nd subject (**8**—**14**) Tonal centre F major

(Alma theme)

DEVELOPMENT
(**14**—**28**)

1st section (**14**—**21**) Tonal centres A minor: E minor: D major-minor

alternating with derivatives of 6:

 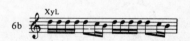

and, later, derivatives of 14:

2nd section (**21**—**25**) Tonal centres C: G: E flat
Pastoral Interlude – with cowbells

3rd section (25—28) Tonal centres B: G minor

RECAPITULATION
(28—36+9)

1st subject (28—33) Tonal centre A major-minor

Motto (Fate motifs) A major/minor
Transition (33+3—35—2) Tonal centre A minor
dovetailing with
2nd subject (35—2—**36+**9) Tonal centre D major
(Alma theme)

CODA
(36+10—end)

Tonal centres E minor: D major: E flat minor: C major: A major

Peroration of Alma material=**42**

II

RONDO
(a: b: a¹: c: a²)

(a) **Primary section** (beginning—**51** or **92**) Tonal centre E flat

25

(b) **1st episode (51—55 or 92—96)**
Part I (**51—53** or **92—94**) Tonal centre E minor
Part II (**53—55** or **94—96**) Tonal centre E major
Pastoral Scene with cowbells

29    30

(a¹) **1st return of Primary section** (abbreviated)
(**55—56** or **96—97**) Tonal centre E flat

31

(c) **2nd episode—extended into development (56—61/97—102)**
Part I (**56—57** or **97—98**) Tonal centre C major
Part II (**57—59** or **98—100**) Tonal centre A major/minor
= Return of (b) Part I
Part III (**59—61** or **100—102**) Tonal centres C sharp minor:
F sharp: B includes return of cowbells and dovetails with
2nd return of Primary subject at **60**—1 or **101**—1

(a²) **2nd return of Primary section treated as Coda**
(**60**—1 or **101**—1—end) Tonal centres B: E flat

III

SCHERZO
with twice alternating TRIO

1st Scherzo
(beginning—**73** or **56**)

Primary Scherzo section (beginning—**66** or **49**)
Tonal centre A minor

Secondary Scherzo section (**66**—**73** or **49**—**56**)
Tonal centres D minor: B flat: A minor

1st Trio
(73—82 or 56—65)

Primary Trio section (73—80 or 56—63) Tonal centre F

Based on derivatives of Scherzo material especially 48 viz.:

Transition (80—81 or 63—64) on Pedal-point A

Secondary Trio section (81—82 or 64—65) Tonal centre F minor

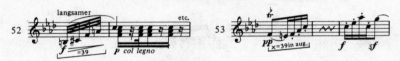

2nd Scherzo
(82—88 or 65—71)

Primary Scherzo section (82—85+4 or 65—68+4)
Tonal centre A minor
Secondary Scherzo section (85+4—88 or 68+4—71) Tonal centres
C minor: A minor

2nd Trio
(88—97 or 71—80)

Primary Trio section (88—95 or 71—78) Tonal centre D
Transition (95—96 or 78—79) on Pedal-point F sharp
Secondary Trio section (96—97 or 79—80) Tonal centre E flat minor

3rd Scherzo
(97—101 or 80—84)

Abbreviated. Tonal centre A minor

Coda
(101 or 84—end)

Tonal centre A minor

IV

EXPOSITION
(beginning—**120**)

Prefatory section (beginning—**104**) Tonal centres C minor: A minor

Motto A—B

Introductory section (**104**—**109**) Tonal centres A minor: C minor: G
Part 1 including return of Pastoral Interlude but with deep bells

plus derivatives, viz.:

combined with further
derivative of 55:

Part 2 Chorale

Part 3 Return of Mottos and linking passage

False Start and Primary section (109—116)
Tonal centres C minor : A minor

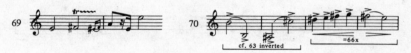

Transition (116—117) Tonal centre A

Secondary section (117—120) Tonal centre D major

DEVELOPMENT
(**120**—**143**)

1st section (**120**—**129**) Tonal centre D minor/major
including development of Pastoral Interlude with cow and deep bells
(a) Prefatory section (**120**—**121**—2)

(b) Development of Pastoral Interlude (**121**—2—**122**)
(c) Return of False Start (**122**—**123**)
(d) Development of Secondary section (**123**—**129**)

2nd section (**129**=First Hammer Blow—**140**)
Tonal centres G major/minor: A major: F sharp major/minor:
C minor/major: G: A
(a) Turbulent development of Chorale (**129**—**131**)

(b) 'Victorious Exultation' (**131**—**133**+4)

31

(c) 'Cataclysm' (**133**+4—**134**)=development of Transition

(d) March (**134**—**139**)=development of Primary section

(e) 'Spiritual Uplift' (**139**—**140**)

3rd section (**140**=Second Hammer Blow—**143**) Tonal centres B flat:
G minor/major: C minor: D minor
including 2nd turbulent development of Chorale

RECAPITULATION
(**143**—**164**)

Reprise of Prefatory section (**143**—**144**) Tonal centres D minor:
C major/minor
Motto A—B

Reprise of Introductory section (**144**—**147**) Tonal centres C minor:
F minor/major
including reprise of Pastoral Interlude with cow and deep bells

Reprise of Secondary section (**147**—**153**) Tonal centres B flat major:
A major
including peroration corresponding with 1st movement at **42**
Reprise of Primary section (**153**—**161**) Tonal centre A minor
including Reprise of Transition=**159**+5—**161**

OVERALL CLIMAX OF FINALE AND SYMPHONY
(**161**—**164**)

= Reprise of (e) 'Spiritual Uplift'   at **161**
        (b) 'Victorious Exultation'   at **163**
      (from 2nd section of development) Tonal centre A major

CODA
(**164**—end)
Tonal centre A minor
(a) Final return of Prefatory section (**164**—**165**)
Motto   A—B = Third Hammer Blow

(b) Threnody (**165**—3 before end)
(c) Tableau—'Fate triumphant' (last 3 bars)
Motto   A (minor chord only)—B

Part 2: Discussion and Analysis of Form

I: **Allegro energico ma non troppo**

1

It can only have been as an act of careful planning that this symphony, which is even more closely associated with Mahler's personal life and philosophy than its predecessors, and which introduces orchestral features of such novelty and originality, should be so much more conventional in its purely formal aspect. It opens with a symphonic Allegro whose basic structure is also the most traditional and clear-cut of any of the work's four movements, being in strict sonata form, viz.:

Exposition: Beginning—**14**   = 112 bars+conventional
                          repeat
Development: **14**—**28**   = 163 bars
Recapitulation: **28**—nine bars after **36** = 88 bars
Coda: ten bars after **36**—end   = 108 bars

This plan immediately exposes the relative length of the development section, a proportional emphasis that is accentuated in its effect during performance by the slow tempo of the central section. The coda is also of unusual stature and importance, making clear that the movement is laid out on the Beethovenian scale of the *Eroica* or *Choral* Symphonies.

2

The **Exposition** is characterized (again like the first movement of Beethoven's *Choral*) by an unusually rich assortment of thematic ideas, especially in the primary section. The section subdivides as follows:

Introductory section: Beginning—**1**   = 5 bars
Primary section: **1**—four bars before **7**   = 51 bars
Transitional section: four bars before **7**—**8**= 20 bars
Secondary section: **8**—**14**   = 46 bars

The **Introductory section** is exclusively concerned with Ex.1 and with its pounding reiterated bass notes sets the march-like character on which much of the movement is based. Only five bars in length, it nevertheless assumes importance through its return at the key points in the structure.

The **Primary section** centres around the home tonality of A minor though with the briefest excursion to and from the subdominant, D. Its main concern is the first subject proper, Ex.2, which it introduces and discusses together with its host of appendages Exx.3–12. A striking feature of Mahler's method is the way in which apparently minor developments of a theme will suggest the basis for new themes which later acquire independent life and character of their own. Thus at **3** Ex.a

graduates via Ex.b

to Ex.8 which, delivered first on the trombone, is one of the more vivid of the subsidiary first subject motifs. At the same time the trumpet phrase Ex.b, significantly cut off abruptly before it can reveal too much of its potential, contains in its first four notes the germ of one of the most important motifs of the Finale, Ex.63.

If technical proof were ever needed of the invincible power of Mahler's personality as a composer it could be best found in his ability to take thematic ideas from the works of other composers, works which no doubt formed part of his everyday repertoire as conductor, and make them unmistakably his own. Exx.8 and 9 are virtually identical with primary themes from Liszt's E flat Piano Concerto and Schumann's *Manfred* Overture respectively, yet they are re-identified here with the style and character of this highly individual mind.

The section ends with a catastrophe and collapse (five bars after **5**—four bars after **6**) in which earlier motifs struggle against the destructive effect of Ex.12 but are all dragged down to the abyss.

The **Transitional section** is formally extremely direct. A violent enunciation of the symphony's motto-themes, Exx.A and B, is followed immediately, and with noteworthy contrast, by the soft Chorale, Ex.13, suggesting calm faith even under severest adversity. The chorale had, from the composer's earliest years, played a prominent part in Mahler's symphonies, but this is the first to have been introduced so early into the symphonic structure. Yet it may be significant that even now this Chorale plays no part in the argument but serves rather as an interlude, returning only once in the movement at the corresponding place in the recapitulation. Nor does it bear any relationship to the far more typically Mahlerian chorale in the Finale, being much nearer to the style and spirit of Bruckner, a similarity intensified at this first statement by the countertheme on pizzicato strings, as discussed in Chapter III (see p.71). One further point should be noted: in both motto themes and chorale the tonality has remained firmly rooted in A minor, without any hint of the modulation often expected of a transition passage leading to the second subject.

The **Secondary section** plunges straight into the second subject proper (Alma's theme, see Chapter III p.71) which bursts in, therefore, without modulatory preparation, in the submediant key of F. The whole section remains in this key during all the three-part-plus-coda formation on which it is built. For the statements of Exx.14 and 15 (which together constitute the second subject proper, although Ex.15 later acquires an independent life of its own) surround a martial, rather jerky development of the Lisztian theme, Ex.8, presented first in inversion and then the right way up. The coda is also based on a reflective version of Ex.14 sounding unexpectedly like a passage from Leoncavallo's *I Pagliacci* (the coda of the love duet in Act 1), which again was certainly a strong element of Mahler's musical subconscious as a result of his work in opera houses.

As the exposition finally subsides, a ghostly reference is heard to the drum-beat motto-theme, Ex.A. This at first leads to the pounding bass of Ex.1, as the first-time bars take the music back to the beginning of the symphony.

If one were to be told that Mahler had prescribed the repeat of a first movement exposition only once before in his symphonies, one's first impulse might be to choose either No.2 or No.4 as the most likely candidate, since both these movements are also built on classical sonata form. On the contrary, however, it is the unconventional opening movement of No.1 which during a later revision was thus extended in a flash of perceptive intuition. On the other hand, the repeat in No.6 seems to have been from the beginning an integral part of the conception. There should therefore be no question of omitting it, as is done far too often in performance with damaging results to the proportions and drama of the work.

3

The **development** is in three clear sections:

Primary development section: **14**—third bar after **21**		= 75 bars
Pastoral interlude: third bar after **21**—**25**		= 53 bars
Resumption of development and linking passage: **25**—**28**		= 35 bars

The **Primary development** begins by taking the drum-beat motto, Ex.A, as its point of departure. On this a *Marche macabre* is built up using Ex.1x and Exx.6–9 together with two new ideas: Ex.16 and a derivative of Ex.6 quoted as Ex.6a. As the bass creeps steadily and chromatically downwards the harmony moves to the dominant minor (E minor), whose arrival heralds a majestic return of Ex.2. Mahler seems to have intended a full-scale episode in the new key, for he marks a change of key signature; but in the event it lasts only eight bars. Ex.2 is treated in such a way as to emphasize the octave leap (bracketed in the example) in both direct and inverted form. The effect of this is also to underline the relationship to Ex.2 of the chorale countersubject from the transition.

At the end of the eight bars the key signature is once more cancelled and the march resumes, again firmly anchored on A minor. The metamorphosis of Ex.6 is carried a stage further by the xylophone figure, Ex.6b, which introduces a further new theme, Ex.17, a melodic strand of the self-fertilizing kind Mahler was past-master at inventing. The whole cantilena from eight bars before **18** to four before **19** is of exceptional interest, spanning as it does the range of Mahler's melodic powers from the Finale of the Second Symphony to the great interlude from the 'Abschied' of *Das Lied von der Erde*, already clearly anticipated by the woodwind:

Ex.c

A new jerky figure together with its inversion comes gradually into prominence but is soon proved to be no more than a distortion of the opening phrase of Ex.14. It is accordingly quoted as Ex.14a but amply justifies its place in the list of themes, as does the inverted form, Ex.14b, the character of the music being radically changed with their appearance.

There is a further change of key-signature to a single flat, but the tonality of D minor is only briefly passed through, the development now gathering pace with an urgent sense of modulation. Ex.7 plays a strong part in the heightening tension, its secondary figure rising instead of falling.

The **Pastoral Interlude** abruptly interrupts the drama, the only link being a gentle statement of the second subject's falling phrase, Ex.14y, on the woodwind. This melodic fragment, seeming at first to have been left high and dry by the instantaneous change of scene, in fact returns from time to time in reflective vein, almost as if Mahler were visualizing his wife strolling amongst the mountain cows on some verdant *Alm*. Indeed the word-play on her name may possibly have suggested the scene to his mind and hence the very concept of introducing the new timbre of *Herdengelaüte* into the symphony, however much he may have allowed himself subsequently to rationalize the mental process (see Chapter III p.78).

Two new motifs are introduced, Exx.18 and 19, belonging specifically to the Interlude, which accompany – or alternate with – the second motto theme, Ex.B, and the Chorale, Ex.13. These themes are first in C and then G, before a return is made to the D that had been held as a pedal beneath seven bars at the beginning of the Interlude, as if still trying to establish itself in keeping with the key-signature. This D being now treated as a dominant, the signature changes to one sharp and another new melodic idea, Ex.20, is quietly intoned in the key of G. So new to the structure does this cantilena seem that it is with pleasurable surprise that one soon recognizes (through a sly intercession on the horn) its simple identity as the inversion of Ex.3. Its phrases mingle with Alma's secondary figure, Ex.15, as the key centre moves – again with a change of signature – to E flat. In this tonality the Chorale is heard once more, this time in full, bringing the interlude to a peaceful cadence into which the main development breaks vehemently with its continuation and closing section.

This, listed above as **Resumption of development and linking passage,** is relatively short and could reasonably be considered *in toto* as a link between the interlude and the recapitulation. Yet it has an important function which is pursued in the manner of a development; that is, to assert and work out Ex.8a as a motif in its own right. As a result, it no longer emerges as a mere off-shoot of Ex.8, as seemed the case at its first appearance during the collapse of the primary section of the exposition (i.e. at **6**) (a full statement of Ex.8 itself abruptly reminds one of the derivation), but with its intervals widened to span an octave it seems to claim kinship with the first subject, Ex.2. This connection is emphasized still further in the actual linking bars (three after **27—28**), where the interval is widened to a tenth, and is indeed cemented once and for all when these bars lead directly to the recapitulatory return of Ex.2. Mahler's thematic material is exceptionally closely integrated in this movement.

In building the last section of his development Mahler creates new passionate melodic strands by augmenting Ex.4a, the highly evocative results being illustrated by Exx.21 and 21a. The Chorale, Ex.13, also contributes to the violent discussion, entering first at a curiously stark moment when Ex.8a is hurled out simultaneously with its own inversion. The Chorale is further repeated, always by the horns in a furious diminution – an unusual and unexpected treatment, as if expressing outrage at being thus overwhelmed.

Many distant keys have been traversed in this terse passage which had thrust itself onto the scene in the far-flung tonality of B major. The key signature, which actually showed the five sharps, has changed to that of G minor during the submerging of the Chorale and with masterly control of chromatic modulation Mahler drives the music up, step by step, to the triumphant return in the tonic tonality of A (**28**) in terms of absolute and unshakable conviction.

4

The **Recapitulation** is abbreviated, especially in the second subject, viz.:

Primary section: **28**—**33** = 48 bars
Transitional section: **33**—three bars before **35** = 16 bars
Secondary section: two bars before **35**—9 after **36** = 24 bars

The **Primary section** begins regularly, except that the actual moment of return is with Ex.2 in the major. This is emphasized by a change of key signature to three sharps, even though this is to last for no more than three bars. Ex.1, whose introductory function has thus been omitted, returns as in the exposition, although the pounding bass notes now create a pedal point on E, suggesting at first an ambivalent tonality before their strongly dominant function reasserts itself. The other first subject motifs then follow conventionally, the section from **29** to **33** corresponding remarkably closely to **2**–**7**. Continual adjustments proper to a reprise are, however, made so that the flow of ideas remains positively in the tonic of A minor, even though in the exposition no actual modulation had taken place.

Hence the returns of the motto-themes and the Chorale are in A as they were before, after the descent from catastrophe which has pursued virtually identical lines despite the very slight extra conciseness (the whole passage in fact occupies forty-eight bars against fifty-one in the exposition). The chief difference of the **Transitional section** lies in the change of orchestral treatment, particularly the magical colouring of the Chorale's return in which the derivative counterpoint is cut out entirely.

Another major change occurs, however, as Alma's second subject approaches; for instead of bursting in, this emerges most subtly out of the repeating phrases of Ex.13, drifting in the process into the tonality of the subdominant D major, in which – complete with signature – it is recalled in all essentials though simplified and without the interpolations of Ex.8. The reprise of the **Secondary section** is thus only twenty-four bars long compared with forty-six in the exposition, a compression which also discards the muffled reminder of motto-theme A that had concluded the exposition. This reference is now left out of the recapitulation, the music passing directly to the coda.

5

The **Coda** might be said to represent the Triumph of Love over Adversity. On this basis it divides into two roughly equal sections:

Introduction and continuation of development = 55 bars
Allusion to Pastorale, peroration of second subject and conclusion = 53 bars

The introduction, eight bars in length, sets out with the pounding bass notes as if a further reprise of the opening might be planned. But the bass notes themselves are now F sharps, and instead of Ex.1 it is a gloomy, sinister statement of Ex.2 on the brass that is superimposed in the key of E minor. Then there is a violent change of mood and tempo, and the music drives savagely on once more with a resumption of the primary development section (**14—21**). The new motif with which this raging vehemence storms in ('wütend dreinfahrend', Mahler himself says) is quoted as Ex.22. Ex.23, which follows, is plainly derived from Ex.2 but is of such crucial significance in its relationship to the material of the Finale (cf. Exx.63, 70 etc) that its working out is the main feature of this section of the coda, partially obscured as it may seem by the mêlée of developing material already familiar from earlier similar passages. The alternately rearing and plunging leaps range right up to an eleventh at one point (Ex.d):

Amongst the many changes of key signature, that of one sharp seems to indicate some stability in the establishment of E minor as a temporary tonal centre, but the music plunges before long into six flats as motifs from the second subject are introduced. These include Exx.14a and 14b for a brief resumé of the jerky martial, central section of the second subject, which had been omitted in the recapitulation.

All the flats vanish as the skies clear for the second part of the coda and C major fanfares against a glistening celesta background recall the mood of the pastorale, Ex.19 being strongly in evidence. This fifteen-bar transition then leads the music to the tonic of A and to the optimistic major mode again for the peroration of Ex.14. Love has triumphed and from here to the end all is jubilation.

II : Andante moderato[1]

1

.As in the first movement, Mahler cast his contrasting Andante in what is *au fond* a strictly classical form, this time that of a rondo. However, the remarkable homogeneity of both the material of the rondo-subject and that of the episodes, as well as the even, unbroken, warm flow of the melodic line, tends to obscure the structural design. Furthermore, a misleading effect is created by the way in which the episodes themselves also break up into sub-sections.

The overall plan is, then, as follows:

(a) Primary Rondo section: Beginning—**51** [**92**]   = 55 bars
(b) First Episode: **51** – **55** [**92** – **96**]   = 44 bars
(a) First Return of rondo theme and tonality: **55** – **56** [**96** – **97**]
    = 15 bars
(c) Second Episode: **56** – **61** [**97** – **102**]   = 58 bars
(a) Second Return of rondo material and tonality: **61** [**102**] – end
    = 29 bars

The most striking features of this movement are, firstly, the length of the primary rondo section, which has indeed something of the expository character of a ternary song with coda, and then a formal characteristic which cannot adequately be presented in a simple plan. This is the way the last two sections of the rondo are dovetailed to form a single arched curve, the transition from the one section to the other occurring during a period of maximum intensity. Indeed the dividing line could equally be represented fourteen bars earlier (i.e. one bar before **60** [**101**]) at the actual point of the return of the rondo theme, even though in a vastly distant tonality, as will be shown in due course. Such a view would have the effect of altering the structural proportions

[1] For an account of the problems concerning the movement order see Chapter III pp.89ff.

41

in favour of the coda (= 43 bars) while reducing the second episode to a length almost exactly equal to that of the first episode and second return alike (= 44 bars). In practice, however, the turn of the corner into the home key of E flat at **61 [102]** is not only clearly perceptible but also highly dramatic, whereas the return of Ex.24 is in the lower instruments and hence partially hidden beneath the impassioned melodic sweep of the violins and upper woodwind. Hence, however aware one may be of the structural design, the true return can only be fully appreciated at the heartfelt re-establishing of E flat at **61 [102]**. There is also an appreciable gain in accepting the shorter proportion of the second return since this acts also as coda, whose reflective quality is strongly pronounced from the moment the home key has at last been reached after the long discursive second episode, by this reckoning the most extended section of the movement.

2

The **Primary Rondo theme** falls into four sub-sections, all except the second centred firmly on the tonic of E flat, viz.:

Principal Stanza: Beginning – **47 [88]**	= 20 bars
Alternating Stanza: **47 – 48 [88 – 89]**	= 7 bars
Return of Principal Stanza (varied): **48 – 50 [89 – 91]**	= 14 bars
Coda: **50 – 51 [91 – 92]**	= 14 bars

The first statement of the **Principal Stanza** is expansive, being based on the discursive melody Ex.24. A subsidiary figure closely related to passagework from the first movement – compare the oboe solo two bars before **46 [87]** with Ex.4x – is developed as a motif in its own right and therefore quoted as Ex.25. The section sinks to a close, unexpectedly in the minor mode, with repetitions of Ex.25 as these merge into further variants such as Ex.25a (again compare Ex.10 from the first movement – these allusions can hardly be coincidental although this Andante has the fewest 'cyclic' thematic links of any movement in the symphony). A cadential phrase arises out of the first bar of the rondo melody which, though not quoted in the schematic examples above since it plays no structural role, should nevertheless not escape attention (Ex.e):

Ex.25a becomes the background to the cor anglais statement, Ex.26, which begins the short **Alternating Stanza** in the key of G minor. The figure x from this melodic fragment treated sequentially leads to the **Return** of Ex.24 in varied form, though back in the tonic of E flat major. A further cadential figure is now introduced which has the character of a new theme, Ex.27.

The **Coda,** apart from a brief reference to Ex.e, is entirely concerned with Ex.25. It is linked to the First Episode by a rising octave in semi-breves, Ex.28, which has been a Mahlerian magic door to new vistas since the days of the First Symphony.

3

The **First Episode** is in two clear sections, 28 and 16 bars long respectively. Of these, the earlier has very much the character of a development, whereas by contrast the second is an interlude, its analogy with the pastoral interlude from the first movement being underlined by the return of the cowbells.

The earlier section is in E minor, which shares with E flat a common mediant, G. Hence through the rising octave link, Ex.28, this note serves as a pivot, the new tonality entering with Ex.25 so that it is the subsidiary section that is developed first. Exx.26 and 27 are prominent, whilst in addition new and allied melodic patterns are incorporated, such as Ex.29 and 30.

The second section is largely atmospheric. E remains the tonal centre though the change to major is very striking, building from bass upwards with harps and a horn call (Ex.f):

Ex.30 has developed into an ostinato against which various elements contribute to the tableau, some motivic and some purely splashes of colour.

Suddenly the warmth drains out of the texture and a chromatic string passage leads downwards to a return of E flat and the rondo-melody, Ex.24, whose figure⌈ x ⌉has played a leading part in the transition.

4

The **First Return of the Rondo theme** is very brief and yet substantial enough to establish itself both as a motivic reprise and as a true home-coming to the primary tonality of E flat, before embarking on fresh and more adventurous journeys. Ex.24 has a new and very affecting descent on the 1st violins, ending with a phrase that refers, consciously or unconsciously, to the first of the *Kindertotenlieder*. The cadential bars (bars 2–6 of p.88 [137]) then extend Ex.24 both in the rhythmic manner of Ex.25 and melodically as shown in Ex.31, this being itself an extension of Ex.e above. The last bar before **56 [97]** stands alone as a modulating link to the following section which begins in C major but behaves as a true modulatory development.

This **Second Episode** can be viewed as being in three clear subsections; the first (in C) is short – only nine bars – passing abruptly to the second, for which the key signature changes to three sharps. This subsection, twenty-two bars in length, is itself in two parts divided by the rising octave, Ex.28; the second part reintroduces Ex.26, though in the atmosphere of calm with which it was played in the early part of the first episode. It remains, as always, in the minor mode – in this instance A minor. The third subsection is by far the most considerable although its actual duration, twenty-seven bars, is not much more than that of its episodic predecessor. Yet by contrast this is in a single span which, moreover, continues in effect to embrace at least twelve bars of the melodic outpouring of the succeeding passage, even though – as has been discussed above – that belongs from the formal point of view to the second return.

Beginning in C sharp minor with yet a further entry of Ex.26, this time in the lower instruments, the music gravitates to the key of F sharp major in which a surging movement develops. Treating F sharp as a dominant, however, the principal rondo theme contrives its hidden dovetailed return in the key of B, which it establishes so firmly and with such vehemence, Exx.25, 24y and 31 being especially featured, that there is a truly dramatic element of piled-up tonality when at **61 [102]** the soaring cantilena boils over into E flat. This is a contrivance of which Richard Strauss was inordinately fond (in the early religioso section of *Also sprach Zarathustra* as well as in more than one of the Lieder he uses it three times in succession so that the tonality comes round full cycle) but Mahler uses it sparingly so that it cannot fail in its emotional impact.

5

With the **Second Return of the rondo material and tonality** the mood of descent into coda is all-pervasive, though especially so after the cadence at **62 [103]** which marks the musical half-way point of the section. Here it is Exx.27 and 30 that are most strongly in evidence, although Exx.26x and 25 both have moments of passionate evocation. There are memories of the ostinato use of Ex.30, though now greatly broken up, presenting the merest whisper of recollection of the pastoral interlude as the movement sinks and fades away in perfect calm.

This Andante is perhaps unique amongst all Mahler's symphonic structures in its uniformity of mood and unsullied radiance. For parallels one recalls inevitably such other wistful escapes from reality as the Andante of the Second Symphony, but even there the episodes contain strong contrasts of mood and texture. Here, however, a welcome and undisturbed respite is provided before the savage onslaughts that lie ahead, for which purpose its revised position is particularly well judged as Mahler, with his acute sense of performance, quickly realised.

III: SCHERZO

1

In the sketches for his Tenth Symphony Mahler wrote at the head of one of the scherzos 'Der Teufel tanzt es mit mir',[1] and so he might well have written here. The last movement of Liszt's *Faust* Symphony depicts the devil not by themes of his own but by distortions of Faust's themes, on the basis of Goethe's famous line for Mephistopheles: 'Ich bin der Geist der stets verneint'.[2] Though less relentlessly true than in Liszt's movement, where there is not a single Mephistophelian motif that cannot be traced back to the Faust section of the work, in this most vicious of Mahler's scherzos the thematic material is to a large extent derived from the first movement.

The mood is alternately diabolical and bitterly satirical, even the

[1] 'The devil dances with me'.

[2] 'I am the spirit which ever negates'.

Altväterisch[3] trio sections wearing mirthless grins as they strut about in deliberately affected mien though interrupted by repeated bursts of harsh laughter.

Although as in the previous movements all the material within the Scherzo is exceptionally closely interrelated, the two trios developing in their own way ideas already put forward during the main scherzo sections, the movement clearly falls into the Beethovenian form of a scherzo with twice recurring trio, viz.:

Scherzo: Beginning – **73 [56]**	=	97 bars
Trio: **73 – 82 [56 – 65]**	=	101 bars
Second Scherzo: **82 – 88 [65 – 71]**	=	74 bars
Second Trio: **88 – 97 [71 – 80]**	=	99 bars
Third Scherzo: **97 – 101 [80 – 84]**	=	37 bars
Coda: **101 [84]** – end	=	38 bars

It will be noticed that the last return of the scherzo is greatly abridged. This is in line with Beethoven's practice in, for example, the Fourth Symphony.

The proportional balance might be considered better preserved by regarding the third scherzo and the coda as a single section, but this is neither in line with the meaning of the music at the juncture of **101 [84]** nor with the character of what follows: for the gradual unwinding of the music which gives it so much the feeling of a coda has also the strong suggestion of a third trio whose momentum has been lost, and which ends by collapsing altogether under the repeated attacks of the fate-motif, Ex.B, leaving the last word with the scherzo's Ex.34x.

2

The **First Scherzo** falls formally into two balancing sections:

Primary Section: Beginning – **66 [49]**	=	33 bars
Secondary Section: **66 – 73 [49 – 56]**	=	64 bars

These are constructed on the pattern of any Beethoven scherzo, as would have been immediately apparent had Mahler cast the music within the conventional repeats of earlier times. In accordance with tradition, the primary section is markedly shorter than the secondary, which modulates and even proposes some new material of its own,

---

[3] Lit. 'old-fatherly', i.e. old-fashioned, though this describes the style less graphically.

before returning to the tonality and motivic work of the opening. This return occurs at the third bar after **69 [52]**, and consists of twenty-seven bars plus a seven-bar link to the first trio.

The **Primary Section** presents the wealth of essential scherzo material, Exx.32–45 corresponding with the host of ideas from the primary exposition section of the first movement. Of these, many of the scherzo motifs constitute Mephistophelian metamorphoses on the lines just discussed. For example, the pounding A's of Ex.32 are palpably equivalent to the pounding bass of the symphony's opening which it also links with ⌐ x ¬ from the motto-theme A; Ex.33 is an extension of the figure ⌐ x ¬ from Ex.1; Ex.34 can be traced back to Ex.2 with its insistent to-and-fro between the notes A and C, a derivation shared, if in retrograde motion, by Ex.38 which is first heard as a countertheme to Exx.33 and 34; Ex.39 has much in common with Ex.11 although the upward sweep is carried further in the original version of the figure; Ex.42 is directly related to Ex.6, a kinship emphasized unmistakably by the xylophone's aggressive clatter, recalling Ex.6b from the later version of the motif in the first movement's development section.

All these themes are firmly established in the tonic of A minor and are welded together into a unified structure that is rounded off by Exx.44 and 45 (the latter perhaps consciously connected with the similar rising octave Ex.28 from the Andante). Ex.44 vacillates back and forth between chords of A (major or minor; this alternation also turns out to be of crucial significance) and B flat, the latter in its first inversion so that in the bass the pivot note is D. With the rising A's of Ex.45 poised above the D on which the figure pauses, the key of D minor becomes a logical tonality for the beginning of the **Subsidiary Section.**

A restatement of the primary motifs, Exx.32, 33 and 38, in the subdominant minor is followed by a linking period of four bars in which the undulating Ex.44 is treated in imitative strands instead of its previous chordal format. This in turn leads to a passage of new material, Exx.46 – 49, centring on the distant tonality of B flat major. Most of these motifs are to play a primary role in the trio sections, where they undergo remarkable character changes although their notes remain essentially the same. The variation of bar-metre in Ex.48 is noteworthy, being rare for Mahler, and anticipating his intended use of a similar technique for the first scherzo of his Tenth Symphony.

The return to the opening, once again in the tonic A minor, occupies twenty-seven bars and culminates in a return to Exx.44 and 45, which are now revised so as to incorporate a violent re-entry of motto B, its major/minor feature heightened by the descending figure ⌐ y ¬ now added for the first time to Ex.45. The earlier major/minor conflict in

Ex.44 whose significance now becomes manifest, has here been transferred to the greater drama of the Fate motif.

This is followed by a seven-bar link to the trio consisting of an extension in diminuendo of the repeated A's, Ex.32, though now rising in a succession of piled octaves which moreover leap-frog with C's added to the A's. The lower octaves then drop away and only the C's remain so as to dovetail with the first oboe phrase of the trio, Ex.48a.

3

The scheme of the movement outlined above (p.46) shows that the trio sections are longer than those of the scherzo proper. In fact the **Trio** is in three subsections, its primary and secondary sections divided by a transition with a motif of its own, viz.:

Primary Trio Section: **73 – 80 [56 – 63]** = 75 bars
Transition: **80 – 81 [63 – 64]**   = 10 bars
Secondary Trio Section: **81 – 82 [64 – 65]** = 16 bars

The apparent disproportion between the Primary and Secondary Trio sections should not lead to a misunderstanding over their relative importance, the secondary section being characterized by the greatly slower Ländler-like tempo which features in other Mahler scherzos, such as those of the Fifth and Ninth Symphonies. The entire trio is in the tonality of F, the primary section in the major, the secondary in the minor.

The themes which constitute the long **Primary Section** are all directly derived from the secondary scherzo section, i.e. Exx.47–49, but whereas they had been strong and self-possessed – amounting even to a single optimistic interlude in the Danse macabre – now they are either mannered or derisive. Ex.48a illustrates the famous *Altväterisch* oboe solo that contains most of the elements used for structural purposes. The figure ⌐ y ¬ is developed to a considerable degree both directly and in inversion. This material is interrupted repeatedly by Ex.47 played *drängend*, that is to say pressing forwards, so that it gives an effect of mocking laughter.

As the section draws to a close, Ex.47's role is usurped by the little twist ⌐ y ¬ which ends Ex.48, treated imitatively in a similarly ribald *drängend*. The timpani breaks in with the pounding A's of Ex.32 and the **Transition** follows.

Exx.50 and 51 give the dragging motifs on which this brief linking section is built. During the last two bars they merge into an inverted

48

variant of Ex.38, over which Ex.33 leads into the **Secondary Section** of which it is a salient motif together with Ex.39, both borrowed this time from the primary scherzo section. Themes specifically belonging to this very concise section are the rhythmic Ex.52 and the augmented stylized version of Ex.39 quoted as Ex.53x.

4

The **Primary Section of the Second Scherzo** runs regularly from **82 [65]** to six bars after **84 [67]**, though the last bars are abridged so that Ex.45 makes no reappearance here. This shrinkage is part of the general plan whereby the second scherzo is already shorter than the first, as shown on p.46. But whereas the primary section is twenty-eight bars long (compared with thirty-three), the **Secondary Section** has no more than forty-six bars (compared with sixty-four bars). Hence it is the latter that has been the most severely cut back, having lost its opening restatements of Exx.33 and 38 as well as the greater part of the passage containing the new material, Exx.46–49, which has only six bars instead of twenty. The purpose of this is plain enough, since it is these motifs that form the thematic content of the trio sections, and the briefest of references is sufficient to establish the formal reprise. As before, it starts with a modulation, this time by way of C minor in which key the return to the opening of the scherzo at first remains. But Mahler now varies the procedure so that although the compression only amounts to seven bars (twenty-two instead of twenty-nine) the effect is of far greater economy. There are short modulatory returns of Exx.44 and 47 leading to a further dramatic re-entry of the basic scherzo themes, Exx.33 and 39, now firmly restored to the tonic A minor. The motto B then returns in its regular position, though sharply reinforced by the rhythmic pattern Ex.52 from the secondary trio section, as well as by a blatant trumpet passage (Ex.g):

The figure ⌐ x ¬ from Ex.g now replaces Ex.45y for the collapse into the link to the trio, this too seemingly compressed from seven bars to only four. But there is an illusionary effect in Mahler's notation, for having arrived at the double-bar and the slower *Altväterisch* tempo he actually prolongs the staccato A's for two further bars before Ex.48a begins, thus expending nearly all his previous saving. This suggests some earlier revision, perhaps a change of mind during the copying out of one of the draft particells. It is only one of many instances where study of the sketches could be of the greatest interest.

5

The **Second Trio** is closely related to the first, viz.:

Primary Section: **88 – 95 [71 – 78]** = 73 bars
Transition: **95 – 96 [78 – 79]** = 9 bars
Secondary Section: **96 – 97 [79 – 80]** = 17 bars

The **Primary Section** of the second trio follows period by period in the footsteps of the first (though based on the key of D instead of F), yet all the details are revised and rethought. This even affects which of the large number of thematic motifs follows upon its predecessor, new successions thus creating fresh patterns out of often-heard motivic fragments, with additional variations of bar-length. Moreover structural cornerstones are re-created with new dramatic *coups* such as the caesura between **91** and **92** [**74** and **75**] which corresponds with – and replaces – the entry of Ex.32 at **76** [**59**].

The **Transition** again uses the mediant of the previous tonality (here F sharp=mediant of D major, compared with A=mediant of F major, the tonality of the first trio) as a pedal point on which to build the chromaticisms of the wailing Ex.51, but when Exx. 39 and 52 reassert the secondary section the tonality no longer corresponds with the earlier passage but slips up a semitone to E flat minor, thus disturbing the original unity of the trio as a whole. Further, the omission of Ex.33 at the end of the transition (cf. two bars before **81** [**64**]) is deceptive, for the **Subsidiary Section** is far more closely linked to the scherzo than that of the first trio, with new and prominent references to Ex.42 as well as to Exx.33 and 34, all sounding oddly macabre in the slow Ländler tempo characteristic of the section.

6

At **98** [**80**] the Scherzo once again returns violently and abruptly. As is discussed in Chapter III (p. 107), Mahler originally left out the *Tempo I subito* which as at **82** [**65**] marks the cornerstone of the two sections, but the passages correspond so closely that there can never have been any misunderstanding. This **Third Scherzo** is greatly cut back in length, amounting in effect to a single-minded build-up to the climax of the movement, Exx.44 and 45 following naturally upon the concise final reprise of the primary scherzo material. There is, this time, no suggestion of formal duality as in the earlier scherzo sections.

The climax itself, however, is quite remarkable. It consists of an eight-bar period built not – as expected – on the searing A major/minor of motto B, but on a viciously orchestrated 7th chord:

This was prepared by means of extending the rising octaves of Ex.45 to minor ninths, so that the A's soar to B flats. Against descending chromatic scales on strings and flutter-tonguing flutes, the oboes give vent to a shrill fanfare-like version of Ex.48x, followed by Ex.51 which, groaning as it too descends chromatically, finally collapses on to a pedal A.

On this pedal the drum-beat Ex.32 starts up in preparation for the **Coda,** where indeed it continues relentlessly for twenty-one bars whether on the timpani or, briefly, pizzicato cellos. Woodwind and first violins play reflectively with the trio material against entries of motto B (whose omission at the climax is thus explained) dropping octave by octave as well as in instrumentation, by way of the horns to end on muted trombones. The first of these entries is heralded by Ex.39, screamed out by the clarinets, the reiterations of the pounding drum-beat being briefly transformed into the variant Ex.52, though after two bars they change back again to the simple regular beat. Exx.49 and 47 also appear as the music quietly moves towards its appointed end, descending to the depths at last to finish with Ex.34x, intoned with slow meaningful placing on timpani and pizzicato basses. Notably the last entry of the motto theme B drops an octave to its minor triad: anguish and irony have passed, leaving behind only despair.

IV: FINALE

1

This enormous movement appears formally more complicated and unconventional than it really is. Apart from the difficulties of immediate perception posed by its sheer length, the complexities boil down to, firstly, the framing slow prefatory introduction and coda sections; secondly, the long threefold development; and, thirdly and above all, the irregular recapitulation which not only reverses the order of first and second subjects but also reaches its culmination in the reprise of material derived less from the exposition than from the central development section.

Reduced to the very simplest essentials the proportions of the Finale appear as follows:

Prefatory Section:
  beginning – **104**   = 15 bars
Introduction: **104 – 109**   = 82 bars
Exposition: **109 – 120**   = 131 bars

First Return of Prefatory Section:
  120 – two bars before **121**   = 8 bars
Development:
  two bars before **121 – 143**   = 283 bars (!) [1.   2.   ]

Second Return of Prefatory
  Section: **143 – 144**   = 17 bars
Partial Reprise of Introduction:
  144 – 147   = 38 bars
Recapitulation: **147 – 164**   = 198 bars

Third Return of Prefatory
  Section: **164 – 165**   = 17 bars [3.   ]
Coda: **165** – end   = 33 bars

In appreciating the structure of the movement during performance it is particularly important not to be misled by the placing of the famous hammer blows, indicated within square brackets in the above scheme. These do not mark the conventional cornerstones of the Finale, the first two occurring within the development, the third in the last return of the prefatory section (see Chapter III pp. 127, 135, 151).

2

The **Prefatory Section** consists specifically of Ex.54 together, on every occasion but one, with the motto themes A and B. Strangely its four appearances are not in the same key, and the one that opens the movement actually starts in C minor, reaching the tonic of A minor only in time for the entry of the mottos. The significance of this will emerge in due course. The whole section of fifteen bars is spanned by the immense curve of Ex.54, the initial rising octave ⌜x⌝ being of primary motivic significance in its anticipation of later themes of the Finale (Exx.55, 63, 70, 74, etc), as well as linking these retrospectively to motifs of earlier movements (I: Exx.2, 23; II: Ex.28; III: Ex.45 and possibly even 37). The phrase ⌜y⌝ of Ex.54, enunciated *ff* by unison strings, is subjected to the violent onslaught of the two mottos which are again in their original timbres of timpani and brass respectively.

The **Introduction,** into which Ex.54 subsides, is in three parts:

Part 1 – Atmospheric quasi-Recitative: **104 – 106**   = 33 bars
Part 2 – Chorale: **106 – 107**   = 16 bars
Part 3 – Return of Mottos and linking passage: **107 – 109** = 33 bars

Exx.55–64 present the material on which, with the exception of Ex.58, the exposition of **Part 1** is to be built. The motifs are enunciated in differing styles and each with its own character – often even its own tempo. Thus when later they are worked into a unified symphonic structure they preserve their identity because of the individuality they revealed at their first hearing.

Though becoming increasingly chromatic in style, the whole recitative-like pre-exposition is based on A minor. The first statement (on the tuba) of Ex.55 is punctuated by vehement entries of Ex.56y (=Ex.39 =Ex.11) and Ex.57. Against a background of Ex.58 (=Ex.18, itself a background figure), Exx.59, 60 and 62 are introduced, these being the future themes of the second subject. Something of the mood of the pastoral interlude from the first movement is evoked here, although the cowbells are replaced (for the time being) by deep church(?) bells. According to Professor Redlich these are indeed intentionally evocative of the church 'as symbol of dogmatic creed', but Mahler left no evidence of this. All he ever actually specifies is the random, unregulated sound of deep, distant bells of undefined but differing pitch. It is by no means unlikely that Mahler's purpose this time was purely one of colour, bells being one of the sounds of a pastoral scene such as he was conjuring up and which he had no doubt experienced when walking with Alma in the mountain countryside.

The peaceful scene is disturbed by a violent upheaval. During a ten-bar period thematic fragments are either hurled to-and-fro (Exx.64 and 55c), rear up through the turbulent textures (Ex.63), or jab out like grotesque distorted fanfares (Ex.56). The confusion then abruptly subsides into the Chorale of **Part 2.**

This is a simple sixteen-bar sentence (4×4 bars) in C minor, the last four-bar phrase modulating to G. (Exx.65 and 66 quote the first two phrases.) The **3rd Part** then breaks in with Ex.39, heralding the motto themes A and B, unusually in the tonality of G (major/minor). The slow twenty-nine-bar build-up then begins, consisting of two balancing sentences (15+14 bars).

The first of these sentences again picks out motifs of the furtive second subject that had previously been broken up by the turbulent section (Exx.61 and 62, the former listed amongst the other second subject material although appearing here for the first time). Indeed the restless background tremolos of that extraordinary passage continue to haunt these fifteen bars.

The second sentence resumes the processional manner of the previous chorale section, though based on new motifs. Exx.67 and 68 are strongly announced simultaneously at the outset and lead to a composite but salient figure that is repeated again and again in slightly varied forms, such as Ex.h:

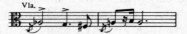

There is no difficulty in tracing the origin of Ex.h back to Ex.62, Ex.59x or elsewhere, yet its individual contribution during the course of the movement is enormous, especially if one regards its identity as still being preserved even when nothing but the rhythmic shape remains clearly recognizable, with every one of its notes perhaps changed, including their relationship to each other. For example, the following figure (Ex.i) on the horns much later in the movement can still be rated as an entry of Ex.h:

After the four strong bars of Exx.67 and 68, Ex.h initiates the eight-bar crescendo that at last connects this long preamble to the Allegro of the exposition, though the climax is delayed by a further return of motto B. This, however, peals out in the key of C instead of in the true tonic of A. There is an analogy here with the finale's opening which was also in C minor for some few bars before arriving at the tonality of A. In fact, as will become increasingly clear in the development and recapitulation, the key of C minor plays a positive role as subsidiary tonality across the spectrum of the whole movement.

3

The **Exposition,** together with what turns out to have been a false start, can be broken down into its component sections as follows:

False start in C minor: **109 – 110** = 16 bars
Primary Section: **110 – 116**　　= 62 bars
Transition: **116 – 117**　　= 15 bars
Secondary Section: **117 – 120**　= 38 bars

The **False Start** is largely concerned with the permutations of Ex.55 quoted as Exx.55a–c (though Exx.55c now appears in quaver-semiquaver notation). With the aid of Exx.56y and 57 the music quickly builds in intensity and shifts its tonal centre so as to lead to the Primary Section in A minor. Shortly before this is reached there is an anticipation of the frenzied version of Ex.55c which, as Ex.71, is to play a cataclysmic role in the transition and thereafter in development and reprise.

The **Primary Section** is by far the most extensive part of the exposition. It is entirely orientated in the tonic of A minor and presents in a martial *Allegro energico* the principal first subject material consisting of Exx.69 (in all essentials a derivative of Ex.55 which itself appears together with its variants, especially Exx.55c), 57, 61 and 70, the last of these bringing with it a number of melodic phrases relating to the Chorale (Exx.65–68).

A stormy entry of Ex.56y (=Ex.39) marks the **Transition**, consisting of Exx.71 and 72 which sweep convulsively over powerfully augmented statements of Ex.61x. The music and the tonality then descend to D major for the second subject.

The **Secondary Section** is relatively brief and again centres around a single key, the subdominant D major. It is in three sections – fourteen bars, twelve bars and again twelve bars in length – which are contrasted in mood, being respectively optimistic, radiantly passionate, and stormy. The cheerful section presents Exx.59, 60 and 62, now in their true role of second subject, against a gaily chattering rhythmic ostinato. Ex.73 then leads to the passionate middle section of which Ex.74 quotes the opening sentence. The stormy conclusion of the secondary section, as also of the exposition, harks back to the drama of the transition, though its motivic origin is at first the typically Mahlerian figure Ex.64 (cf. the first movement of Symphony No. 2) against which trumpets pile up a theme (Ex.j) derived from Ex.59:

A rearing augmented form of Ex.63 then heaves to and fro against Ex.73, there is a direct reference to the transition, and the entire fermentation collapses into the first return of the prefatory section with which the development begins.

4

The **Development** once again falls into three clear sections, whose proportions are as follows:

Section 1: **120 – 129** = 107 bars (including first return of prefatory section)
Section 2: **129 – 140** = 143 bars
Section 3: **140 – 144** = 41 bars

As this shows, the principal substance lies in the central section which carries the main burden of the working-out. Of the sections on either side of it, much of the first has a strong introductory character while the third is a terse, even precipitous, link to the recapitulation.

Nevertheless the **First Section** is by no means inconsiderable, and itself falls into four subsections, viz.:

(a): **120** – two bars before **121** = 8 bars
(b): two before **121 – 122** = 21 bars
(c): **122 – 123** = 13 bars
(d): **123 – 129** = 65 bars

(a) presents the first return of the prefatory section, though this amounts to hardly more than an allusion. Its motif, Ex.75, is none other than Ex.54 inverted except for the opening octave leap that remains upwards as in Ex.54x. The downward octave has, however, already been snarled out during the first bars of the subsection by eight muted horns with their bells in the air.

(b) gives a brief development of the introductory section in which this time both the cowbells and the deep church-bells are heard. Ex.58 (and similar patterns) persist in harps, celesta and tremolo strings, so that the pastoral atmosphere is recalled. As in the original introductory section itself, thematic fragments appear and vanish like ghosts, notably Ex.55b in augmentation on the tuba, Exx.57 and 73, and Ex.59 – though the opening figure of this theme is changed so that it now recalls Ex.19 and thus refers directly back to the pastoral interlude of the first movement.

(c) corresponds to the false beginning of the exposition. Its thirteen bars are entirely concerned with Ex.55c (as before, in quaver-semi-quaver notation) and Ex.56y. It also remains rooted on D minor as has been the whole development up to this point. Its last two bars, however, provide an abrupt modulation, presaged by the increasingly wild outcries of Ex.56y, flinging the music into F sharp major in preparation for subsection (d), with which the development proper may be said to get under way.

(d) primarily develops the second subject material, discussing first the fanfare-like motif Ex.59 in a manner strongly resembling the *Trauermarsch* from the Fifth Symphony, and then passing on to a long and impassioned section based on Exx.73–4. Numerous other motivic figures join in the mêlée, including fragments from the Chorale and vehement outbursts again recalling the Fifth Symphony. A climax is built up, the crest being marked by the **First Hammer Blow.**

5

In all the preceding development passage the tonality has remained centred on D, whether minor or, later, major. Now, however, the function of the note D is changed, pivot-like, to wrench the music out of its tonal stability in the hectic maelstrom that succeeds the first hammer blow. This **Second and central Section** of the development should again be subdivided in order fully to understand its sequence of thought and dramatic purpose which is to some extent programmatic. This purpose is integral to the message of the movement and thence to the whole symphony, and in this respect the return of its various events, though in a different order, will be of primary significance when the time comes in the reprise. The five subsections, then, can be summarized as:

(a) Turbulent development of Chorale: **129 – 131**	=28 bars
(b) 'Victorious exultation': **131** – four bars after **133**	=21 bars
(c) 'Cataclysm': five bars after **133 – 134**	=12 bars
(d) March development: **134 – 139**	=61 bars
(e) 'Spiritual uplift': **139 – 140**	=21 bars

Section (a) is as important in its violent or feverish figures of accompaniment (beginning as Ex.77 which alternates with rushing scales, leading in their turn to an important variant of Ex.67y quoted as Ex.78) as in its impassioned development of the chorale. This starts with a derivative in augmentation of Ex.67, quoted as Ex.76. The connection with Ex.78, which emerges from the background as if in answer, is clear enough and leads to a cumulative discussion against descending scales. Ex.j, still on trumpets, is heard pressing through the thick texture that overflows into section (b), the tonality rising, through a sequence of pedals each a fifth higher than the last, to a radiant A major.

So bright and optimistic is **Section (b)** that the label given to its programmatic significance in the above summary should not seem too fanciful, though it applies principally to the first half. Ex.80 runs its all too briefly jubilant course followed by a *cantabile* version of Ex.h, with Ex.60 often added to its tail. The sky then clouds over gradually as the tonality shifts again to F sharp, first major then minor, followed by an icy slip down to F minor. Ex.61 tries to reassert itself in the bass instruments but it is too late; the horns and brass break in brutally with the cataclysmic Ex.71a, whose figure $\boxed{\text{x}}$ presents yet a further elaboration of Ex.55, described in the example as Ex.55d.

Section (c), short as it is, is so overwhelming that it wipes the slate clean and all is left clear for an entirely new section of working-out to begin. The moment of climax is marked by a terrifying brief hiatus capped by a C major cadence, the violence of whose drama cannot be exaggerated. The analogy is with the Last Trump and March of All Creation from the finale of the Second Symphony – also, it will be recalled, in C minor.

The March itself constitutes **Section (d)** and is by far the longest and most fully-worked passage in this central section of the development – itself the longest and most complex central section of the Finale – this in turn again the longest and most elaborate movement of a symphony which is also the centre point of Mahler's entire output. It can, therefore, however much with hindsight, be viewed as the kernel of Mahler's creativity, and that this should be a march is wholly consistent with the regular appearance and reappearance of the march throughout his works whether in song or symphony. Exx.81–83 present its principal motivic basis, Ex.82 being of primary importance since its jerky rhythm forms an ostinato lying beneath the greater part of the march. This can be seen to derive from as far back as the introductory section of the whole finale, the first statement of Ex.82 being actually incorporated into the outburst that included Exx.55c and 64. Thereafter the rhythmic pattern common to all these examples has constantly appeared in the exposition and especially in the development where, as Ex.77, it featured in the passage following the first hammer blow. Brutal interjections of Exx.39 and 55d attempt in vain to disturb the inexorable drive of its progress and Ex.55d returns to its basic shape of Ex.55a which now takes over the role of principal motif.

The tonality swings from C to G major and Ex.68 rings out in varied and various forms, the rhythmic phrase now tending in opposite directions (Ex.k):

It will be seen that where the bracketed figures go down they previously went up, and vice versa (see Ex.68). Ex.k battles against renewed attacks of Exx.39 and 55d until, with the aid of Ex.h, victory is won and the music attains to the security and simplicity of **Section (e).**

The last struggle has again wrenched the tonality away from any fixed centre; furthermore, out of the heaving of Ex.k on all the deep brass instruments a shift has taken place so that the moment of victory is in the tonic key of A, as well as in the optimistic major mode.

Short as it is, this last subsection of the central development is in two clear and virtually equal parts. The first, broad and song-like, is based on Ex.84, which, deriving from Ex.75, develops in glowing sonorities the inverted form of the first prefatory theme announced at the very beginning of the development. The second part arises out of the background references to Ex.h and corresponds almost identically to the build-up that closed the introductory section (see p. 54 above and cf. pp. 158/9 of the score). Instead of heralding the Motto, however, this time the cadence resolves on to the **Second Hammer Blow.**

6

As before, the hammer blow marks the threshold of a new phase of the development, this time the short **Third Section.**

During the last ten-bar build-up, the tonic A major tonality has been undermined by modulation over a chromatically ascending bass; so that, when at last the grand cadence proves to be poised above the note A, the ear willingly accepts this now as a dominant in preparation for a new passage in D minor. The resolution is, however, a surprise, for at this further hammer blow the music plunges into B flat, this key also to be quickly modified and turned by the pealing chorale Ex.67

(blazed out by the heavy brass with their bells raised) towards a tonality centred at first around G.

The frustrated D minor cadence is nevertheless only delayed, for after renewed and hectic turbulence has led to a headlong working out of Exx.75 and 78, rushing ever more precipitantly through a series of chromatic modulations, the last cadence of the whole long development does in fact plunge down on to a heavy sustained low D.

7

The **Recapitulation** is the most unorthodox section of the movement and has misled many commentators. In particular not only are the first and second subjects reversed in order but, when the reprise of the first subject does come, its strong forward drive leads to a reprise of elements from the development, for which very purpose it has been delayed. The form and proportions of the recapitulation can be presented as follows:

Second Return of Prefatory Section: **143 – 144** = 17 bars
Partial Reprise of Introduction: **144 – 147** = 38 bars
Secondary Section: **147 – 153** = 67 bars
Primary Section: **153** – four bars after **159** = 16 bars
Transition: five bars after **159** – eight bars after **160**
  = 16 bars

Reprise of dramatic events from Development, namely:

(a) 'Catastrophe': nine bars after **160 – 161** = 8 bars
(b) 'Spiritual uplift': **161 – 162** = 16 bars
(c) 'Triumph over adversity': **162 – 163** = 21 bars
(d) 'Victorious exultation': **163 – 164** = 8 bars

} = 53 bars

This last composite section constitutes the climax of the movement and symphony alike in its programmatic optimism, destined to be so rudely overthrown by the catastrophic events of the tragic coda.

The very beginning of the recapitulation is already irregular in being superimposed upon a foreign pedal-note. For, as we have seen, the development has ended with a headlong cadence in D minor and the bass D is sustained continuously beneath the **Second Return of the Prefatory Section** until the ninth bar, by which time Ex.54 has felt obliged to enter willy-nilly, and moreover in C minor as at the opening of the movement, regardless of the tonal conflict. The D therefore fades away, having lost its tonal significance during the first bars of the new section under the onslaught of the superimposed 7th chord:

which has so strong a character that by the time the motto themes enter also in C minor the listener has completely forgotten that the music was actually in quite a different key and has been pushed into C minor by sheer brute force.

But in the original prefatory section the motto themes had entered in the true tonic of A minor so that here is another irregularity, and their retention of the subsidiary key of C emphasized the importance of that tonality, with which – it should be remembered – the whole vast movement began. Moreover, since the motto portion of the prefatory section has now remained in C minor, so the reprise of the introduction now takes place in that key instead of in the tonic A minor.

At first the events of the **Reprise Introduction** are essentially the same as before. Ex.55, with occasional interruptions from Exx.39 and 57, leads to a return of the pastoral music dominated as ever by Ex.58, though this time both species of bells are heard – the cowbells and the deep church bells. Out of this mood-picture Ex.59 rises as before, but Ex.73 can also be heard in wistful interjections. There is no upheaval, but instead an ethereal combination of Exx.59 and 62 on muted brass *pp* and very high clarinets against shimmering violins. The background Ex.58 returns one last time to accompany an impassioned entry of Ex.54 in inversion on the solo violin, and two further poignant entries of Ex.73 as the cowbells ultimately fade away into the distance.

Then suddenly the air has cleared; the reprise introduction is over and the recapitulation proper is firmly in progress, beginning however in the key of B flat with the **Secondary Section** and its group of themes Exx.59y, 60 and 62 presented by the oboe. It corresponds very closely with its exposition statement which was also given to woodwind and also accompanied by a quaver pattern played by other woodwind. (Here they are simple quavers whereas before they were triplets, but this is a mere variation of detail.) As before, the strings intrude on the wind ensemble and quickly – even impatiently – take over the texture; but in the same way as the mixed tones of different wind instruments in the exposition are now replaced by a solo oboe, so the strings begin by introducing solo players. The texture then quickly builds up, as Mahler has a surprise in store.

For the second subject, which has just been so innocently and delicately handled, is now blazoned forth as a culminating hymn by the massed brass and percussion sections of the outsize orchestra. There is in fact a strong analogy with the corresponding peroration of Alma's theme towards the end of the first movement (at **42**) which in its turn had looked back to the Fifth Symphony (see Chapter III p. 85). The timpani figure, the use of augmentation, the heraldic instrumental setting, all suggest that the symphony has reached a grand culminating moment.

But the pause breaks off abruptly in mid-phrase as if Mahler suddenly realised that this is all far too soon. The strings burst in passionately (Ex.j against vehement descending scales of Ex.64) and drive the music furiously forwards.

The next thirty-two bars are a tremendous reprise-extension of the latter part of the exposition (**119–120**), the mood being of unrestrained energy and passionate optimism. Already by the third bar the harmony has plunged down a semitone from B flat to the tonic A major and in this jubilant key not even Motto theme A (thundered out threateningly by the second timpanist) can exercise restraint.

At **153** the delayed **Primary Section** of the recapitulation is reached in the full flood of the continuously surging symphonic drama, the key turning to the minor mode for the purpose so that in this respect at least the structure is entirely correct according to the strict tenets of classical form. Yet so great is the momentum that the upper strata of the orchestra continue with the second subject material for a further four bars, while the lower instruments firmly establish Exx.69, 55c and 57 exactly as at **110**.

Yet the overlap is not entirely in the forward direction. The return to the first subject had already been presaged by Ex.61 on the trumpet at **152,** so that when it recurs during the four bars before **154** it acquires the character of an after-phrase.

The primary section, remaining now at last firmly centred on the tonic A minor, follows closely the argument of the primary section of the exposition and arrives duly at the transition, the fifth bar after **159** corresponding exactly with **116**. There are even exactly the same number of bars (62) between **153** and the fifth bar after **159** as there had been between **110** and **116**.

8

In the exposition, the essential purpose of the short transition section was to interpose a moment of crisis (Ex.71), from which the resulting turbulence subsided to a point at which the second subject could emerge. But with the reversal of the first and second subjects in the recapitulation, the **Transition** – coming as it still does at the end of the primary section – now takes on an entirely different role, that of actually leading upwards to the **Reprise of dramatic events from the development** which forms the very crisis itself. Ex.71 therefore no longer forms a part of the transition reprise, although this too is almost the same length as before. Instead, Ex.55d (no longer catastrophic in character when thus isolated from Ex.71) and Ex.72 lead to a leaping development of Exx.67 and 68, which together with an augmented and doubly augmented form of Ex.55d build towards a majestic climax. Before this can be reached, however, a savage interruption occurs in the shape of a formidable return of Ex.71a, now without Ex.55d, and in the absence of that motivic link rendered strangely more terrifying than ever before. Ex.72 resumes, and the whole disruptive, chaotic melisma brings the structure down in ruins; Ex.73 is greatly in evidence together with its own form in diminution, plunging down octave by octave.

But, phoenix-like, Ex.84 rises from the ashes, later to be joined by its inversion in the creation of a new, noble edifice in the confident home tonality of A major. New entries pile upon each other, now in blocks of consecutive triads; even Motto theme A has lost its ferocity, as the horns declaim a victory march based on Ex.79 against the jubilant strains of Exx.73 and 74, together with the inverted form of Ex.84. A carillon is added on the horns (Mahler does not use the real bells – they had quite another nostalgic power of association) to ring out against repeated assertions of Ex.61x; the drama seems at an end, the hero has surely triumphed.

9

For the last time the seventh chord rings out – and based on a low A of unprecedented sonority. So the **Third Return of the Prefatory Section** brings a full statement of Ex.54 in the key of A. In agonized foreboding the oboes enter a bar later with the inverted form of Ex.54 starting on the tritone E flat and descending so as to come to rest on the note A.

The fears are well grounded, for the Prefatory section not only brings both Motto themes back, the dreaded themes of malignant fate, but their entry is reinforced by the third and fatal hammer blow. This time the drama has truly ended – and in tragedy.

Death and defeat at the moment of greatest exultation is the cruellest of all, and is here the more shattering for its terseness and speed of impact. After so long a struggle the end is brought about in a mere seventeen bars.

The rest is epilogue. The **Coda** consists of a moving threnody for the brass on a contrapuntal treatment in broken phrases of Ex.55, though now the octave seems to be always falling. One last time, however, it manages to rise, giving a final mournful statement of Ex.55 as it was first heard at the outset of the finale. Then, with a guillotine-like shock, the fate motifs crash out again, but motto B no longer has its major/minor alternation. For there is no longer any question of threat – the worst has happened; only the minor chord rings out. It is Fate that has trimphed as Fate always must. A brief comma, and the symphony ends numbly with a soft pizzicato A punctuated by brass drum.

Seemingly short on paper, the funereal coda is in fact perfectly porportioned, viz.:

(a) Third and Final Return of Prefatory Section: **164 – 165** = 17 bars
(b) Threnody: **165** – three bars before end   = 30 bars
(c) Tableau – 'Fate triumphant':   = 3 bars

The symphony is utterly convincing and the handling of the enormous structure masterly. Its creator had good reason to be himself moved by it; that he was so superstitiously terrified of its message is sad but wholly characteristic. Unlike Strauss, there was in Mahler's mind no division between life and art. The two were inextricably intertwined and in his works Mahler reflected everything that he was. It is a controversial issue whether the Sixth Symphony shows the artist at his greatest; that it reveals the man most completely there can be no doubt.

Gustav Mahler: etching by Emil Orlik, 1903

Chapter Three

Comparative Commentary

Mahler subjected each of his symphonies to wholesale revision as the result of his experience of rehearsing and performing them in public. He could be reduced at times to utter despair on hearing his first version of a symphony, and would work like a maniac thinning, changing, clarifying the lines or the instrumentation until he felt more confident that his message would be properly transmitted. Many of these revisions, such as those of the First and Fifth Symphonies, are immensely thorough and amount to hardly less than entirely new versions (a fact that leads to endless confusions between different – and often mixed – sets of scores and orchestral parts) though, remarkably enough, once the final score was reached the changes were never structural. Mahler seems to have been unusually sure-footed where the proportions of his mammoth edifices were concerned.

However radical in all other respects his alterations may have been in one work after another, none are as comprehensive as those he made in the Sixth Symphony. These revisions can best be discussed on a page-by-page basis, while adding comments on other interesting features as they arise. In this connection the first Kahnt edition of Mahler's original version of the score will be referred to as K1, and the later revised printing as K2.

I

p.3   All but one of the editions agree in giving p.3 as the first page of music (pp.1 and 2 being the title-page and the copyright note of the publishers C. F. Kahnt respectively). The exception is the Eulenburg miniature, edited by Redlich (Eul.), which renumbers the pages from 1 onwards; to bring this into line it will be necessary to subtract 2 throughout the page references in the following commentary.

Mahler's original instrumentation list preceding bar 1 curiously indicated the celesta as being 'in F'. This instruction, later removed, is of particular interest.

In the first place it in no way corresponds with the similar indications for transposing instruments, even though the wording is identical. Mahler's notation for the celesta follows the customary practice of writing an octave below actual pitch and this symphony is no exception. Clearly the indication referred to the range of the instrument he required. Yet he only writes from:

to which corresponds with the five-octave

German instrument, such as the Schiedmayer, which

has the compass: to and is thus in no

sense 'in F'. This enigmatic mark has, however, disappeared already by the first revised score (K2), so whatever Mahler first meant he soon thought better of it.

It is interesting that whereas he does say that the celesta should if possible be doubled or even trebled ('womöglich' – he writes – 'zwei oder mehrfach besetzt') he leaves the number of harps undefined, merely stating 'Harfen'. In the *Orchesterbesetzung*, on the other hand, two harps are listed, which conflicts both with the 'mehrere' (several) on p.84 (133 in K1) and with the specifically stated '4 Harfen' on pp.140–1, i.e. at Fig. **96** (**79**) of the Scherzo (pp.116–17 in K1). Redlich in Eul. ingeniously solves the problem by listing '1. und 2. Harfe (*beide doppelt besetzt*)'.

The revised score added an asterisk with footnote to the Heerdenglocken (cowbells) to the effect that for performance in the theatre these should be played off-stage. Curiously the instruction is suppressed in the Erwin Ratz 1963 Revidierte Ausgabe (Ratz) without comment or explanation.

The changes in instrumentation begin immediately. All the woodwind entries on this first page are removed in toto, the few lines needed to complete the harmony being added to the already divided strings. A *crescendo* (probably omitted through an oversight) is added to the side drum in bar 3, i.e. ahead of the strings.

pp.4/5   The double bar and repeat sign attract attention at once. In the First Symphony, the only other in which

68

Mahler repeated his exposition, it was a far shorter and less conventional section than we are dealing with here. For all its forward-thinking and novel features the Sixth is in many ways the most traditionally built of all Mahler's symphonies.

The weighty principal subject cannot have made its proper effect, for Mahler reinforced all its contours, especially the downward octave leaps on the horns and the figure of the third bar on three clarinets. All three cymbal clashes are removed; it was certainly too soon for this effect, but the climax at bar 6 is emphasized by a timpani roll. The three trombones are reduced to a single solo instrument and the violins approach their *fff* at the bar before **2** no longer with the expected *crescendo*, but unusually and imaginatively with a *dim*.

Like the trombones, the trumpets too are reduced to a solo player at bar 2 of the lower system of p.5. Mahler's plan had always been to use a huge orchestra with five-fold woodwind, eight horns, six trumpets and four trombones as a tutti force, but although the revised score still shows thick bands of colour like the unison oboes at **2**, Mahler had realised yet again the importance of contrast through the use of single instruments.

pp.6/7

In bar 5 the subtlety of resting the horns ahead of the lower woodwind and heavy brass proved imperceptible and they are brought back into line.

At **4** the six horns in unison must have proved overwhelming for they are reduced to four, and the emphasis of the viola entries enhanced with acciaccaturas, a favourite Mahler device. The trombone entry of one of the chief subsidiary themes (so disarmingly close to a subject from Liszt's Piano Concerto in E flat) is entrusted once more to a single player lest it obscure another new motif on violins and clarinets (the one virtually identical with a theme from Schumann's *Manfred* Overture).

It was unfortunate that Professor Redlich wrote in his Foreword to Eul. that it 'offers a corrected and revised text . . . its numerous misprints and editorial ambiguities . . . have been rectified'. The missing ♮ to the clarinets' C in bar 6 is only the first of such errors, none of which were in fact corrected when Eul. was printed.

pp.8/9   All the percussion on these two pages is removed with the exception of the timpani roll on the last bar of p.9, which is, however, brought down an octave to the low E, a splendid improvement. The oboes are instructed to play with the bells up, another Mahler speciality. The difference it makes to their stridency of tone is extraordinary.

pp.10/11   Various *retouches* can be seen on these pages, the percussion being again drastically reduced. Alma Mahler wrote in her Memoirs of how she rushed home sobbing after a reading rehearsal of the Fifth Symphony on account of the over-persistent percussion writing which obscured the thematic beauties of the music, and how Mahler subsequently struck out the offending battery of percussive effect, convinced by her passionate outburst. The episode could more legitimately have applied to passages in the Sixth Symphony than the Fifth, which was never so heavily and relentlessly overscored as its successor, and one cannot help wondering if Alma's memory played her false.

             The upward rushes on the woodwind are vehemently doubled by violins followed by cellos with greatly enhanced fervour, and at **6** the violent undulations of the clarinets and bassoons are underlined by the 1st violins, answered by the 2nds whom Mahler would certainly have placed to his right on the concert platform. Since the violas, cellos and basses all take up the figure in turn already in the first version, Mahler must have wondered why he had not thought of adding the violins from the start, so logical does the revision seem.

pp.12/13   At the first bar of p.12 the great Motto theme of the entire symphony, with which indeed it ends, enters almost casually as part of the transition material. In the event it was clearly too matter-of-fact, for Mahler stepped up the shrill side drum roll to a pair of players, matching the already doubled timpani figure.

             The piercing alternation of major and minor triads which jabs out over the harsh drum beats is again a motto of programmatic significance to the whole symphony. It was moreover an obsession with Mahler, for its appearance in his work can be traced as far back as the coda of the Second Symphony's funereal first movement, there as here given to oboes and trumpets. In turn this may very well have originated from the parallel progression in the coda of the *Marcia funebre* of Beethoven's *Eroica* Symphony (bar 228), its poignance already there so fateful. These mottos, major-turning-to-minor triads and savage drum beats, are both hurled out at the climax of this Sixth Symphony, the terrible moment of the third hammer blow, towards which its eighty-minute span moves forward with unabated intensity.

The Fate mottos, as they may then legitimately be called, give way at this their first entry to a Brucknerian Chorale in the woodwind that, already marked **pp**, Mahler marked down even further to **ppp**. It is indeed hard to bring a band of ten or more wind players down to such a point of refinement. At the same time Mahler stepped up the pizzicato counter-figure based on the first subject (see p.4, bars 1 and 2) from **ppp** to **p**, adding accents to nearly every crotchet. Whether or not it is coincidental, the result of subjecting the first theme to this treatment in diminution and inversion is to give it a startling resemblance to the principal theme of Bruckner's Fifth Symphony, where in the last movement it is also used as a countertheme to a chorale:

pp.14/16   Alma Mahler wrote of the Sixth Symphony: 'After he had drafted the first movement he came down from the wood [i.e. the hut in the wood where Mahler always composed] to tell me he had tried to express me in a theme. "Whether I've succeeded I don't know; but you'll have to put up with it." This is the great soaring theme of the first movement . . .'– that is, the theme of these three pages, repeated even more expansively in

The ravishing Alma Schindler with whom Mahler fell so passionately in love, photographed in 1898 by Gustav Klimt

pp.18–22, constituting the second subject of the movement's sonata design.

Certainly Mahler was determined to make sure that this theme would stand out from the swirling background, for he added the 2nd violins to the 1sts in glowing unison and in the bar of **9** sent the violas soaring up as well. At the same time he lightened the background with a few subtle suppressions of horns, clarinets and of course percussion, which had again been vastly over-used.

The harps, too, which make their first appearance at this point, are redistributed much as Mahler was to do in the Seventh Symphony, dividing them so that each can give more verve to just the top or the bottom line than if both were trying to play the whole passage as originally prescribed.

At the third bar of p.15 Mahler's revisions show the first of an important series of rubato variations to the tempo of this Alma theme. The two 'Gehalten' bars before **9** give a needed moment of preparation before the renewed outburst of passion, as well as allowing time for an extra touch of delicate colour provided by two new harmonics supplied by the 2nd violins.

pp.17/18   Here the revisions move towards simplifications of colour and clarity of outline. The removal of the horns makes the trombones stand out more starkly against the strident band of unison woodwind whose rising slurred leaps are now reinforced – in addition to the violins' pizzicati – not by triangle but glockenspiel. The pizzicati of the lower strings have also gone, increasing the effectiveness of their entry two bars before **11**.

pp.18/22   With the entry of Alma's theme Mahler again sought to thin out any extraneous detail, while reinforcing the surging melody whenever possible. He also seems to have had trouble with the celesta, which is hardly surprising. His unusual mark in K1 (consisting of a wavy line after the L.H. chord) to indicate that the player should thump away with both hands together was obviously neither clear nor sufficient. In the revised version he changes the instruction from 'mit beiden Händen' to the more explicit 'mit Zuhilfenahme der linken Hand' and changes the semiquaver figuration to a series of triplets or demisemiquavers. Nevertheless, although one can watch the player working away like mad it is rare that any sound from that most delicate and soft-toned of instruments penetrates the violent impetuosity of Mahler's musical portrait of his beautiful and adored Almschi.

Pages 20–22 continue the rubato revisions of which the first appeared on p.15. The succession of *Zeit lassen* and *poco rit.* indications culminating in the great gesture at the first bar of p.22 are all clear attempts to set down on paper the way Mahler himself interpreted the passage. They result in an ebb and flow of tempo that is the essence of Mahler's style and quite a different matter from a conventional *poco a poco rit.* for which it is sometimes mistaken.

As for the climax, this is scrupulously prepared by the excision of most of the percussion on pp.20 and 21 including, interestingly, the timpani *f* quaver with which the roll on the last bar of p.19 had ended. The feeling of fulfilment must not be anticipated and the roll with its *crescendo* ends in mid-air. The reversed trombone dynamics are also a valuable guide to interpretation.

And when at last the crest is reached there is an added 'N.B. ' with one of Mahler's directives to future conductors, that on the second crotchet the whole orchestra should be raised up, as it were, a splendidly graphic instruction for a hiatus in the flow of tempo resulting from the effort involved.

Lastly at the bar before **13** one may notice in the revisions of the 1st trumpet and 2nd horn an emphasis of phrasing characteristic of Mahler ever since his rewriting of the First Symphony. Already in K1 there are many passages, especially in the Andante, in which the normal phrasing of two slurred notes, by which the second is naturally shortened slightly, is exaggerated to read:

Here the necessity for this had at first escaped him.

p.23

The revisions during the dying phrases that conclude the exposition concern the emphasis of these entries (both horns and clarinets are marked up from *p* to *mf* or *f*), as well as the lightened background at their moments of entry. One may delight in watching Mahler notice an ambiguity – it is only at the second time round (i.e. after the obligatory repeat) that the 4th oboe changes to cor anglais – and ensure that the printers amend the instruction.

pp.24/25

The changes in the first-time bars naturally correspond with those on p.3.

With the arrival of the development, the demoniacal elements that are to be such a feature of the Scherzo already make their appearance. Here Mahler found he had made contrary miscalculations: on the one hand the clarinets' mocking development of the symphony's introductory figure was altogether too tame, and is intensified with the addition of acciaccaturas to their sharply articulated tonguings as also to those of the bassoons; but Mahler also discovered that he had underestimated the bitter penetration of the xylophone whose clatter he was introducing for the first time into a Symphony, just as he had recently been witnessing Strauss's pioneering use of it in Opera (under the name of 'Holz-und-Strohinstrument') for the highly-coloured orchestration of *Salome*. As will be seen also on pp.28 and 30, Mahler realised that his enthusiasm for this new colour had outrun discretion.

On p.25 the structure is clarified in various ways: by the addition of a quaver rest in bar 3 for the melodic instruments, thus bringing the new motivic entry into sharper relief; by reducing the horns, who double the downward plunge in bar 4, from four to two – certainly four horns were too unwieldy; and by taking a number of necessary steps to ensure that the trilling figure in basses and bassoons should not escape unnoticed. The abrupt cessation of the side drum two bars earlier than originally planned was indeed a clever way of focusing the attention.

pp.26/27

Like the percussion, the brass is often thinned out, as with the trombones and tuba in the first two bars of p.26. Conversely, the string colour is added in bars 5 and 6. Perhaps the effect had been starker than necessary so early in the argument.

At **16** Mahler solved what must certainly have been a confusion of omission. The original score had shown clearly enough that the 1st and 2nd trumpets were to retain their mutes until **18** on p.30, but musically this gave rise to some improbable mixtures of tone-colour. The new instruction 'Dampfer ab . . . offen' on p.27 makes far better sense.

pp.28/29   Here the principal concern is once more for greater restraint in the percussion department. But at the fourth bar of p.29, whilst removing the trumpets and doctoring the violin lines, Mahler became concerned lest the vehemence of the music over so many pages should lead to a build-up in tempo. Indeed, the new marks need plenty of time if they are to be scrupulously followed; and since the conflict with the steady fortissimo of the woodwind makes the variations in dynamics of the violins their primary contribution (one may notice *en passant* the restoration of the 2nds in bar 5) it is clear that the new indication *Nicht eilen* (don't hurry – an injunction Mahler inherited from Wagner) is to be taken very seriously – to the point of holding the tempo back slightly.

pp.30/33   Again the trilling figure needed spotlighting; so the violas are summoned to the support of the cellos just for the single bar 3 before **18**. In the fourth bar of **18** the cymbals are removed, just as they were in the fourth and sixth after **17**; but in the exactly parallel bar two after **18** they still survive. Surely this is an oversight and they should either be removed here too or retained two bars later, since this passage is an intensification of its predecessor, bars 3–6 after **17**.

Page 30 is in any case not problem-free since in recasting the horn parts Mahler left the ties for 5th and 6th, which originally led to minims at the fourth bar of **18** just as in the bar before. The hairpins now lead nowhere and should be removed.

The xylophone part is simplified and the brass cut down but there are also some interesting string additions. The marking up of all the *spiccato* and *col legno* passages was very necessary.

pp.34/35   The addition of the cellos to the trilling figure at the third bar is in line with earlier *retouches* and immensely exciting, but it is remarkable that Mahler thought it worthwhile to strike out the doubling flutes in bar 2. This seems to be part of a plan to introduce their colour gradually, for when they do enter two bars later – all four of them on the high F – they are marked *p* instead of *f*. Mahler's sensitivity to the finest grades of the orchestral kaleidoscope was unique.

In bar 7 of p.34 Professor Redlich noticed the careless engraving of the trombones' hairpins, common to all versions, but instead of shifting them a little to the left (so that they would lie centrally under the note rather than partially during the rest) he decided that they were best replaced by *fp*. In the event, this cavalier piece of editing was doomed: the printer merely removed the hairpins, leaving the *f* behind and so rendering the footnote and reference in the Critical Commentary meaningless.

Redlich also noticed the redundant ties in lower woodwind, clearly a survival from some very early sketch in which they must have followed the cellos and basses. These ties are already removed in Ratz.

With fig. **21** we reach a historic moment in music. Here Mahler interrupts the onward drive of his development section to introduce a contemplative pastoral scene somewhat similar to that of the First Symphony. But here he goes further; whereas the First Symphony makes the standard orchestral instruments imitate sounds from the countryside such as the cuckoo, in this episode he brings to his orchestral forces actual cowbells which are directed to be placed in the distance.

This novel and unconventional feature not unnaturally gave Mahler a degree of heart-searching on both ethical and practical grounds. Although it could be argued that the effect was no more than an extension of his habitual use in his symphonies of every external influence of his earliest background and recollections (the call of the cuckoo, military fanfares, the strains of gypsy bands, and so on), he became acutely concerned lest so pictorial a device might be liable both to misunderstanding and to misrepresentation in purely practical terms. One wonders what he would have said had he known that

77

through Webern's devoted adoption of his brain-child in one of the *Fünf Orchesterstücke* Op.10 a link would be forged, with the total acceptance of cowbells as part of the exploitation of exotic percussion devices from every walk of life and from all over the world that was to characterize a whole new school of composition.

For, to Mahler, the introduction of a new colour such as this was not by any means exploration for the sake of extending frontiers or widening the scope of the orchestral palette – it was an intensely private manifestation; and he might well have found its wider exploitation an invasion of a very personal sanctuary, which he himself would only once more visit (in the Seventh Symphony) though with what purpose he chose never to reveal.

With the printing of the revised score, therefore, he added a lengthy footnote, on the one hand outlining in greater detail the required effect with some directions for its accomplishment, but on the other issuing a strongly worded warning against reading into it any programmatic significance. For all the powerful associations inevitably called to mind it is, he says, to be regarded as no more than a technical device.

Such barriers, built around his innermost thoughts, were, however, an open invitation to subsequent research; and scholars have been delving ever since into the psychological purpose which led Mahler to this pioneering stroke. Redlich, for example, believed that one elaborate but plausible interpretation of the distant grazing cows 'as sounds, penetrating into the remote solitude of mountain peaks . . .' was derived from a one-time explanation by the composer himself.

It was, nevertheless, typical of the down-to-earth Strauss to use this symbolic device, pioneered by his introspective colleague, to represent nothing more nor less than real cows grazing on a mountain slope in his pictorial *Alpensinfonie*.

In conclusion, on a purely practical note it has to be admitted that despite his footnote, Mahler did not solve the problem of how exactly he wished the cowbells to be played (nor is this the only practical detail of the symphony that he left unsolved, as will be seen). They are sometimes fixed rigidly on a bar and struck randomly with a soft beater; but apart from the potential damage to the delicate bells this is an undesirable method and quite inferior in its effect to slinging them on a long string which can then be quietly shaken. In the score they are merely indicated by a wavy line, viz.:

pp.36/39

However symbolical they may be, they must have seemed real enough; for Mahler, in giving indications of dynamics, writes for them histrionically, as it were, i.e. instead of *cresc.* or *dim.*, when adding some extra injunctions into the revised score, he wrote *näher kommend* ('coming nearer') and *sich entfernend* ('going further away'). The necessity for these embellishments (at p.36 bars 1/2 and p.37 bars 6/7 respectively) must early have become apparent in the first performances, during which the naturalism of the pastoral scene may have seemed static with the mock cows remaining obstinately fixed and unvaried. They would thus have been too readily associated in the listeners' minds with the prosaic sight of the orchestral percussion player standing in the wings in front of his row of slung bells.

Here again Mahler added the direction *Nicht eilen*, though for a different reason than on p.29 where the savagery of the march rhythm would allow for no ameliorating hurry. In this idyll-like oasis it is the mood of tranquillity that must not be disturbed; both the descending bass clarinet and the chorale of the horns and trombones need leisure in order to make their true effect, especially as the major-minor Fate motif is dynamically reversed, a point easily lost if too quickly passed by. This is pure scene-setting by a master of theatre, albeit a composer who never in his life wrote a stage work.

Mahler's feeling for the smallest detail of atmosphere is remarkable. The successions of trills on violas and 2nd violins is already highly imaginative background tone-painting: in performance he found his exact knowledge of the required effect betrayed by imprecise notation. Once more only an explicit footnote would satisfy him, despite the adding of slurs to the new edition: the players had been breaking the sound between each trill, and this was damaging to the stillness of the scene.

In their lower register the 3rd and 4th flutes proved unable to give enough tone against the *forte* trombones when leading the second round of little fanfares. No fewer than three bassoons in unison, themselves marked *f*, were necessary to put right this miscalculation. Mahler's impatient ardour is no less apparent in his *retouches* than in his original act of creation.

On p.36 during the five bars before **23** it is easy with hindsight to perceive how the tremolando 2nd violins give virtually no harmonic support to so broad a band of woodwind melody, and the extra thickening of the 2nd and 3rd clarinets seemed necessary for the logic of the passage.

Mahler's insistence that this central calm must above all be kept in strict time proved, in the light of actual performance, to have been misconceived. It was precisely too great a rigidity of tempo that disturbed the magical sense of hushed tranquillity. The elaborate superscription warning the conductor not to drag, to keep firmly to the main tempo, is therefore entirely jettisoned in the revised score, which on the contrary adds *sehr ruhig* to the possibly misleading *grazioso* at **22**.

pp.40/41

The idyll is rudely interrupted. In fact the revisions show that Mahler found it hard to make the shock severe enough. Both the dying strains of the chorale with its atmospheric background and the violent resumption of the development section proper are further exaggerated in their opposite ways in order to intensify as far as possible the poignance of transition from nostalgia to the relentless violence of reality.

Particularly interesting in this respect is Mahler's division of the 1st and 2nd violins, who now play together for a whole eight bars, though in each group the outside players slur while the inside players take separate bows to increase the attack on each note. Here, yet again, lest his intensions and notation be doubted, the anxious Mahler spells it out in a footnote.

At **25** the flutes are rested in the revision for three

bars (they would have been inaudible in any case) in preparation for their long unison *fortissimo* low C sharp, a fascinating effect which penetrates without difficulty in the otherwise bare middle texture, though Mahler (taking no chances) doubles them with four oboes marked *piano* to avoid as far as possible the reediness of low-pitched oboes.

pp.42/45

These last pages of the development (the reprise is reached at **28**) show few changes in K2. The violins' divisi is continued on p.42, plus extra accents, and the orchestration is clarified at the third bar of **26** with the completion of the 2nd violins' motivic entry. At the same time one cannot help wondering whether the retention of their hairpin before the new *ff* was an oversight. Before the minim rest it had been logical and characteristic against the prevailing crescendi, but in the changed circumstances it looks doubtful, though admittedly not impossible with Mahler.

At three bars before **27** Mahler adds a favourite portamento swoop to the violins, and at the fourth after **27** he gives to the eight horns what amounts to a new counterpoint, even though the notes are contained within the existing woodwind and string lines. He must have been excited when he noticed the possibility of this brilliant extra imitation. One wonders, however, that he thought it important enough to move the *Immer streng im Takt* a single *beat* to the left so that it coincides with the violins' entry, instead of standing at the barline. That the admonition itself is necessary, however, admits of no doubt: this is a stirring moment and the temptation to forge onwards into the reprise could be hard to resist.

pp.46/54

The rhythmic difference in the bar before **29** between the cellos and all other instruments with the theme is an obvious misprint left uncorrected by both Ratz and Redlich.

Many of the revisions in this fairly exact reprise are similar in character to those in the exposition but some points remain worthy of comment, such as the re-disposition of the percussion on p.46. The idea of continually differing percussion effects was certainly interesting, but the revised version that delays the triangle and cymbals by a bar so that they come together with, instead of preceding, the timpani is stronger and less complicated (the bass drum is removed altogether). The second and third bars of **29** are curiously rethought: the brass phrase is reduced to a single trumpet together with two out of the eight horns (ties were left hanging in horns and trombones, only the former being noticed and deleted by Ratz). Moreover the violas and cellos break off in mid-phrase, leaving only the three brass instruments to finish in their weakest register. On the other hand the 2nd violins' isolated pizzicati are reinforced by 1st violins, so that their fortissimo will without difficulty cap the snarling reediness of the four oboes. Mahler was pleased with this effect for he now introduced it also at **31** on p.50 to even greater advantage, using octave double-stops.

The change of a deep percussion climax to a high one at **29** is again carried out at the corresponding place four bars after **30** with the substitution of cymbals for bass drum, and the martial sounds of the side drum are continued at the second and sixth bars of **31** in place of the not very remarkable low brass and timpani.

As before, the percussion is greatly reduced, including in particular the sacrifice of the tambourine. Indeed, this new tone colour was to be entirely thrown out, as will very shortly be seen.

pp.55/57 The transition chorale-passage must have caused Mahler some anxiety for he changed the colouring substantially. All the woodwind except flutes supported by a single low clarinet are cut out of the opening bars, while the strings and celesta are made more prominent and consistent, the former now all playing pizzicato. In marking the strings up from *ppp* to *p*, however, Mahler overlooked the *sempre ppp* at the last bar of p.55 which survived into K2 and its corresponding orchestral material, as did the omitted 2nd violins' accidentals in the preceding bar, both causing confusion and error until rectified in Ratz.

The unreality of the scene is intensified at **34** by the muting of the horns and trumpets, but the linking bars to Alma's second subject are emphasized by a new *sostenuto* mark four bars before **35**, as well as by the clearer singing qualities of a single horn, instead of four, the part of the lower horns now being transferred to *espressivo* cellos.

pp.57/60   The revisions to the greatly abbreviated return of the second subject are all designed to reduce the tendency to over-statement, the change of the last cadential climax at **36** to a sudden *piano* being particularly striking. In accordance with the requirements of this new effect, the *a tempo* is moved forward by half a bar and four horns now join the lower strings in leading off the first of the dying after-phrases, but the fall-away on the violins in bars 2/3 of p.60, once marked *grosser Ton*, is changed into a *diminuendo* to *pianissimo*.

pp.60/63   Menace is added to mystery with the removal of the **pp** drumroll at the beginning of the long coda, the timpani now reinforcing the soft pounding of the basses and contrabassoon. Line-stresses are also added to the trombones; here all is stealth not jauntiness. At **38** the *col legno* effect is transferred from the strings to the birch played on the wooden rim of the bass drum (*Ruthe – auf Holz*). In addition the tambourine is ousted altogether and moreover plays no part whatever in the revised version of the symphony, its jingling perhaps seeming too frivolous for this intensely serious and ultimately tragic work.

The *L'istesso tempo* is removed from the beginning of p.63 (it is hard to see what it was doing just exactly there), and the xylophone adds its clatter to woodwind trilling as in the early part of the development. Indeed its omission here in K1 looks almost like an oversight.

pp.64/69   Bearing in mind how the brass colour is to be featured at the climaxes of this strenuous coda, Mahler set out to economize in the earlier tutti pages. It can have been no easy matter to find the right timbres for a section of some eight pages (pp.61–9), during which the mammoth orchestra is fully engaged in a continuous *f–ff*. But in rethinking the trumpet parts on pp.65–7 the muting directives have gone awry. Mahler's intention seems to have been to clarify the distinction between the unmuted tone, represented by a single solo player, and the muted in the hands of the 3rd (or 3rd and 4th). But at bar 5 of p.65 he inserted a new *Dämpfer ab* (mute off), in preparation for the brass climax on p.68 where for the three bars before **41** all the trumpets are unmuted, forgetting that the 3rd and 4th players have still the passage on p.67 to play *immer mit Dämpfer*. After this entry there is indeed a new *Dämpfer ab* (new because Mahler had originally mixed his colours by keeping these players muted at the climax, though the further *mit Dämpfer* four bars after **41** suggests a possible slip of the pen), so that the redundant mark on p.65 may well be a simple, though confusing, misprint.

Another practical detail aggravated by thinning the brass concerns the clarinets. In taking over the trombone chords, together with bassoons and lower strings, they are given very much less time for changing back from the A clarinets that had been briefly used to enable the 2nd and 3rd to produce the low C sharp, a note not on the B-flat instrument. Mahler had, however, given the players no more than a single bar to pick up the A clarinets in the first place, so that this becomes hardly more than an intensification of a problem no doubt tackled as players find most convenient, whether by keeping to a B-flat instrument with the low extension-key or by changing to the A over a much longer period.

The clarifications of texture at **40** bring everything into sharper relief: the woodwind tearing off short at their octave C sharp in the bar before **40**, their doubling of the violas taken over by the bright tone of the 1st trumpet; the grotesque tremolo of the woodwind is isolated to just the second bar after **40**, where it is far more obtrusive than in its original position and thus becomes a positive assertion instead of a mere background effect. Moreover, the horns no longer reinforce the muted trumpets (whom they must surely have drowned) during bars 3 and 4 after **40**, but instead now play together with the trombones for the whole of the period beginning at the up-beat to the fifth bar.

The single *f*, however, which has survived at the point of their original entry, now represents a sudden drop in dynamic, perhaps intentionally in order to retain the dramatic *crescendo* back to **ff** in the following bar.

pp.69/70   Clarification continues with a sharpening of contrasts. After the brutality of the wind-band with its blaring brass, the sudden magic of **41** is enhanced by the removal of the tremolando 2nd violins (the celesta being allowed its moment of glory undoubled) as well as by the use of the stopped horn tone, which in *f* at a fairly low register virtually corresponds in volume with the *pp* open quality that it replaces and to which it hands over so effectively at the fourth bar.

Here the 2nd violins now enter, their soft tremolo in its turn replacing the undulation of the four flutes as well as the celesta which, like the flutes, drops out for two bars before rejoining as part of the general *crescendo*.

At the fourth bar of p.70 the trumpet's reference to the second subject's opening phrase, anticipated by many a false entry during the preceding bars, at last jubilantly completes the statement. But the passage takes the instrument too low in its compass to make a truly triumphant effect unaided against so penetrating a harmonic background as is shown in K1. Mahler accordingly cut back the sustained chord of the horns and clarinets as well as of all the low instruments. (Strangely, however, the clarinets do still enter with a piercing *ff* in the next bar.) Furthermore, as the trumpet reaches the lowest notes of the phrase it is now doubled by the cellos, their rich *forte* reinforcing the climax. In the following passage the imaginative dividing of the 1st violins, half arco, half pizzicato, is an interesting revision giving extra sparkle to the massed woodwind's jerky figure.

p.71   The peroration (Alma's theme in augmentation) is so similar to a triumphant moment – also in A major – in the Fifth Symphony that it seems hardly possible that it could be coincidental (see pp. 86 & 87).

The analogy between the two climaxes is made even stronger by the isolation of the timpani in the revised version through the removal of the doubling lower woodwind and strings, these having their turn on p.72, which is rendered the more effective for being preceded by the new *dimin . . . p* in the percussion. The deletion of the cellos and basses also allows for the isolated pizzicato *ff* A at the *pesante,* a fine dramatic stroke.

[Symphony No. 6]

80

[Symphony No. 5]

87

pp.72/3 The substantial alterations on p.72 once more show the result of the creator being his own interpreter. It would be hard to fault the execution of Mahler's design as carried out in the first version, yet the changes show the impatience he must have suffered when trying to bring it to life, standing on the rostrum in front of his bewildered and hard-worked players, none of whom were in any position to sympathize or to understand what could be the matter: the *drängend* was starting too soon, it must only happen a bar later; the woodwind were not coming across, even though three clarinets playing on C instruments (more strident in tone) had their bells raised – the support of violas was needed. Then the effect of the trombone chorale four bars before **43** was ruined through the ear being satiated with their tone-colour during every preceding bar – horns could take over for at least four bars. But why have eight horns on the theme anyway? The extra weight only prevents the *drängend* from getting off the the ground – it would be time enough to introduce the majestic eight-horn quality after **48**. The change of key of the hammering figure five bars before **43** lacked incisiveness – both tuba and timpani must make a special appearance in just that single bar, especially since the cellos and basses, who have been playing *arco* from the beginning of the page, are relieved of their original pizzicato entry.

What remains in doubt, however, is the phrasing of the violins in bars 3/4 of p.72, when compared with the corresponding bars, four and five after **43**. Yet if slurs are added to match, the phrasing of the new 2nd trumpet solo, whose answers are also without slurs, then becomes uncertain. At the same time there is admittedly a parallel consistency in the slurred imitation of the low woodwind and strings at the last bar of p.73. Perhaps Mahler intended the difference, curious as it may seem, for it survived the publication of the revised version K2 which carefully corrected a number of similar places during these last bars of the movement.

pp.74/5 The most notable changes on pp.74–5 are the removal both of the violas and of the doubling of the bass line originally shared between 3rd trombone and tuba. The

1st and 2nd trumpet parts are also re-thought, their unnecessary thickening of the 2nd violins' tremolo giving way to a couple of pointings of horn phrases. Two bars before **45** the raising of the 2nd violins to the higher octave in unison with the 1sts caused the accidental loss of the 1st violins' hairpin, which has sometimes given rise to misunderstanding. It is, however, restored in Ratz.

p.76 On this last tumultuous page of the movement the bass trombone and tuba are removed from the hammering figure, their lumbering weight only impeding the renewed impetus after the hold-up just before **45**. A misprint in 1st violins at bar 3 is set to rights (but like those on the preceding pages left uncorrected by Redlich in Eul.). The outstanding revision, however, concerns the final phrase of all, whose notation is changed from:

to the much stronger:

the germ of which is to be found in the trombones and tuba. In addition, even greater emphasis is added to the overwhelming jubilance and optimism with which the movement ends, by the substitution of strong bow strokes for tremolo in the upper strings during the second last bar and by adapting the phrases of all the lower instruments to join the heavy brass in what is now a mighty unison on the last four notes. So emphatic is this that Mahler was even able to dispense with all the extra percussion (apart from timpani) that originally reinforced the very last note.

The page by page analysis here arrives at one of the fiercest controversies still raging over this ever most problematical of Mahler's symphonies: that is to say, the order of the two middle movements. Briefly the history of this particular confusion is as follows: Mahler originally planned the symphony with the Scherzo placed second, and the Andante third; however, it was never played in this form since at its première on 27 May 1906 at Essen under Mahler himself the transposition of the movements had already been made, as is proved beyond dispute by the detailed review of the performance in the *Dortmunder Zeitung* of the following day.

For Mahler's reaction, even during the rehearsals, had been to realise that the Scherzo was too similar in style and dynamism to follow directly upon the enormously strenuous twenty-two-minute opening movement. Equally, for the Andante to precede the long slow introduction that opens the monumental Finale was not really satisfactory, whereas by reversing the order the necessary contrast and relief on both counts was solved at a single stroke.

But the publishers of this symphony, C. F. Kahnt of Leipzig (who were also the publishers of the *Kindertotenlieder* and the *Sieben letzte Lieder*) had by this time printed and put into circulation both the full and octavo orchestral scores, in which Mahler's initial intention of placing the Scherzo second was naturally still adhered to. Accordingly, on the composer's instructions, Kahnt prepared a detailed printed slip that was henceforth to be stuck into every copy of the smaller-sized score, reading:

Die Reihenfolge der Sätze in der
6. Symphonie von Gustav Mahler
wird folgendermassen bestimmt:

I. Allegro energico, ma non troppo. (22 Min.)
   Heftig, aber markig.

II. Andante moderato. (14 Min.)
   (in der kleinen Partitur als dritter Satz bezeichnet).

III. Scherzo. (11 Min.)
   (in der kleinen Partitur als zweiter Satz bezeichnet).

IV. Einleitung und Finale. (30 Min.)

C. F. Kahnt Nachfolger

However, the piano-duet arrangement that was made by the eminent composer-conductor Alexander von Zemlinsky appeared slightly later[1] and there was just time for the movement order to be reversed, the Andante coming second and the Scherzo third, even though it is perfectly clear from internal musical evidence that Zemlinsky's arrangement is in all other respects of the first version, described here as K1.

[1] It bears the plate number 4649, whereas the orchestral score has 4526.

As for the large-sized score, this was withdrawn and completely re-prepared in accordance with the extensive revisions Mahler had also immediately put into effect. In due course this was then re-issued in its altered guise, though with the date and plate-number unchanged. No new small-sized score (the word 'pocket' or 'miniature' is inapplicable since it measured $10'' \times 7''$) was ever produced, and to the last the study scores continued to carry this original superseded version.

The orchestral parts had, moreover, also been withdrawn and re-engraved including the reversed order of the two movements, as a result of which in full score and parts alike the rehearsal figures were altered in accordance with what was now the definitive version. This is the version here referred to as K2. The figures in the Scherzo, originally running from **46 – 86**, and those of the Andante from **87 – 103**, now ran from **63 – 103** and **46** to **62** respectively.

So matters remained until fifty-two years after Mahler's death, although for some time before the 1939-45 war the study score had itself ceased to be in print and copies of the symphony in any form were thus as much a rarity as performances.

In 1963, however, the Internationalen Gustav-Mahler-Gesellschaft published a new score, which, forming part of a whole new *Gesamtausgabe* edited by Erwin Ratz, was largely based on the revised version. But in addition to a few minor corrections, the main feature of this edition was the combination of the K2 text with the original movement order (although in deference to the only available orchestral material the rehearsal figures were retained as in K2, if out of order as far as the appearance of the score itself is concerned).

This act of substitution Ratz explained in his Revisionsbericht as being justified by what he describes as the 'unfortunate practice hitherto over the matter of the movement order', and he takes it upon himself to propose that Mahler only reversed the order in the first place 'to some extent under pressure' and that 'he had, however, soon recognized the destructive effect of the change and put back the original order'.

Lastly in 1968 the first miniature score of the symphony was published, by the Zurich branch of Eulenburg, with editings supplemented by a long preface and analysis by Hans Redlich. This, however, reverts to the text of K1, though with one or two minor corrections of Redlich's own. The Scherzo and Andante thus also remain here in their original position, moreover keeping the original rehearsal figures.

In his preface Redlich does try, unlike Ratz (who merely makes wholly undocumented assertions such as those quoted above), to sort out the evidence of Mahler's revisions, including that of the movement order. But he, too, takes for granted Mahler's 'intention to revert to the original sequence of movements' and so inevitably the validity of his scholarship is equally undermined through lack of documentary evidence. In the event, the four paragraphs of Redlich's section entitled *The Textual Problem* are full of vague terms such as 'must have', 'probably', 'possibly' or 'evidently'.

The truth is that we simply do not know. Although it is widely believed that in the last years before his death (though only then) Mahler gave performances of the symphony – some say in America though this is very doubtful – with the original movement order restored, evidence is still lacking that can give substance to preferences and opinions based on such beliefs.

Hence there can hardly be justification for reversing Mahler's known and published second thoughts, well grounded and based upon his practical experience in the concert hall. As in my own performances, therefore, this survey will continue with the Andante moderato.

II

p.77
(=p.126)[1]

The opening melody of this exceptionally beautiful Andante has some extra bowings added in K2. Mahler's bowings are a source of dispute and controversy between leader and conductor on every occasion and in every work. They are often highly inconvenient, sometimes even frankly impractical: but they are so intimately bound up with Mahler's intensely personal style and with the sound of his passionate orchestration that it is hardly less than irresponsible to interfere with them more than is absolutely necessary.

Here in particular the new bow-marks show a re-thinking of the 1st violins' tone quality. The normal way to play a melody such as this is to begin it up-bow, and then in the second half of the first full bar to take new bows for the stressed notes. This, however, would be too extrovert an interpretation. Yet to use fewer bows was to risk the beauty of the cantabile being swamped by the accompaniment, even though only the 1st violins are marked unmuted.

So Mahler struck out the 2nd violins for the whole of the first three bars, dividing the violas to take over their

[1] It will be necessary now to refer to the rehearsal figures and pagination of both K2 and (in parentheses) K1.

harmonic line. A down-bow can now begin the movement, giving it a firm start while still allowing for
economy of bows in the unfolding of the melody. Then
the entry of the 2nd violins in bar 4 is re-marked up-bow,
so that while still playing in unison with the violas as far
as the notes are concerned they deviate in the bowing,
thus making a real and identifiable contribution with
their change of bow at the crotchets in bar 5. Accordingly the 1st violins are themselves given an extra bow
and the slur is broken in bars 4-5, both to allow for the
increased weight of the accompaniment and to give
more character to their phrasing.

On the last bar of the page there occurs a comparatively
rare revision of the actual composition. For the horn to
move down on the last beat together with the oboe and
clarinet was not very interesting. It would be better
for it to move independently at the beginning of the
next bar; in this way the horn note-changes all take place
on strong beats and the part-writing gains in individual
character.

p.78
(127)

At the up-beat to **46 (87)** the melodic flow suffered in
K1 from yet another sudden drop in dynamic, the fifth
in six bars, with two more **pp** *subito*s to follow three
bars later. A smoother link would also bring in the
tender after-phrase to greater advantage; hence the little
hairpin added in K2 to oboe and clarinets, not to be
confused with an accent in the clarinets' part on account
of the inexact spacing: where Mahler did want a stress
he made it quite unambiguous, as the *sf* in the bass-
clarinet shows.

Four bars before **47 (88)** K2 clears up a misreading by
the restoration of a missing slur in the clarinets, and on
the last bar of p.78 (127) Mahler adds a *sehr hervortretend*
to the cor anglais' solo, already marked with a series of
crescendo hairpins. The basic *p espr.* in fact refers, as so
often in woodwind solo playing, to the style and tone
required rather than to the true dynamic. The opening
piano cor anglais solo in Janáček's *Taras Bulba* fails in its
effect at anything less than a *molto forte*, yet the player
must, and can, create the impression of playing *piano*.
Here, although Mahler's six background wind instruments do not produce anything like the rich blanket of

string tone against which Janáček's cor anglais has to contend, the four flutes are unexpectedly opaque and the player does indeed need to project in just the way that Mahler's 'coming very much to the foreground' suggests.

pp.79/80
(128/9)

Three bars after **48** (**89**) another revision of composition, again for the horn, incorporates the little turn that is to become one of the salient motifs of the movement. Apart from its motivic importance, so natural does the revised reading sound that it is with genuine surprise that one returns to K1, or to Eul., recalling the lame, unremarkable line of the original version. In K1 it is at **55** (**96**), during the return of the passage in condensed form, that the little figure first appears, combined simultaneously with the reprise of the opening melody, where it is moreover reiterated in both the second and third bars of the phrase. The decision to introduce it already at the first statement – after **48** (**89**) – while still keeping it with its further elaboration at the return, was a brainwave. Both this and the change in the horn parts discussed on p.93 above are amongst the few revisions listed by Redlich in his 'Critical Commentary' to Eul.

A characteristic series of revisions now begins to appear. In the first two bars of **49** (**90**) Mahler adjusted the melodic upbeat both in the 1st violins and in the horn's answer in order here too to exaggerate the phrasing in the manner quoted on p.74. Although this stylized phrasing is so all-pervasive in the Andante as to represent a motif in itself (see Exx.25 and 25a), its overall adoption in every possible circumstance seems to have been something of an afterthought, perhaps dating only from Mahler's lay-out of the music in full score. For it is far from consistently carried out and, even in K2 and Ratz, passages have survived in which it has been omitted in error. For example, Mahler forgot the violas in the first bar of p.80 (127) whereas at the identical return of the passage on p.88 (137) it is the cor anglais and the horn that escaped his attention; all these instances could thus legitimately be brought into line.

pp.81/2

The thinning out of the harmonics around **51** (**92**) shows something of the time-consuming problems Mahler must have encountered at rehearsals. Already in the first movement of the Symphony No.1 he was writing very high harmonics for some of the lower strings, but here he went a stage too far.

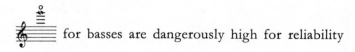 for violas, 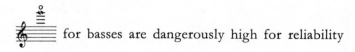 for cellos, and particularly

 for basses are dangerously high for reliability

and on the basses in particular very woolly in quality. It is curious in this context that Mahler wrote the cellos in the treble clef at actual pitch, contrary to his usual practice of using 'old notation' (by which the notes sound an octave lower); whereas conversely, in the basses, he uses the treble clef continuing to sound an octave lower just as they do in their normal bass clef notation. Confusing though it may seem, most composers write treble clef harmonics for basses at actual pitch (cf. Sibelius's *Tapiola*, Stravinsky's *Agon*, etc).

The new injunction *nicht schleppen!* on p.82 (131) is more far-reaching than it may at first seem. Despite its numerous episodes, this quasi-Rondo movement is exceptionally homogeneous and lacking in strong contrasts. For this reason, Mahler became anxious that, apart from two essential corners of the design (the sections around **56** and **59** (**97** and **100**) and the closing bars) the conductor might all too easily be tempted to wallow in such extended melodic sections while enjoying the nostalgic beauty of their contours. Hence the scatterings of *nicht schleppen!*, *fliessend*, and *etwas drängend*[1] on pp.82, 87 and 97 (131, 136 and 146), 90 and 93 (139 and 142), 94 and 98 (143 and 147) respectively, in addition to the already copious collection already to be found in K1.

pp.83/4
(132/3)

A few dynamic changes are all Mahler found necessary in these pages. In particular the **pp** in place of the accent-like hairpin in 1st violins at their re-entry in the fifth bar of p.84 (133) enables the new colour to emerge imperceptibly from the flutes.

---

[1] 'Don't drag', 'flowing', 'somewhat pressing on'.

pp.85/7
(134/6)

The second section of the episode arises out of the first with the sudden reappearance of the pastoral scene with celesta and cowbells. This time, however, harps are added and in quantity (*mehrere*, says Mahler); from the beginning of the movement the plural word 'Harfen' had been consistently applied to the single written part with the clear implication that at least two are to be used. Here even more must have been envisaged, though no exact number is given. In any case this shows that the '1 und 2 Harfe' listed in the *Orchesterbesetzung* is patently out of order.

The cowbells are now directed to be played no longer offstage but within the orchestra itself. In the revision they are made more intermittent, while on the contrary the fluttering 1st violins are strengthened both by the cancellation of their instruction to take mutes and by the reinforcement of four trilling flutes. The horns' dynamics on p.86 (135) are slightly underlined and one seemingly inoffensive *p* cymbal stroke has disappeared, one might hazard, by a slip of the pen, for it was well-placed.

An important confusion Mahler failed to clear up concerns the high 1st violins who, as the pastoral scene fades away, begin a series of impassioned utterances of one of the principal transition motifs. But as one turns the page in the middle of a tied top F it is discovered that this now ties over to the upper line only of a divided section. The orchestral parts reproduce the passage exactly as it appears in the score but it is probably just an oversight. One logical reading would presumably be to make only the outside players of each desk enter in the bar before **54 (95)**.

p.88
(137)

The variants on this page concerned with the return of the E-flat opening have already been discussed above,[1] apart from the new *zurückhaltend* at the third bar of p.88 (137), which, in contrast to the earlier revisions designed to keep the movement flowing, allows the return of the main section to linger even more nostalgically. The single cadential $\frac{3}{2}$ bar which links the music to the episodic development in the unexpected tonality of C major is, however, given a rise and fall in place of the

[1] See p. 94.

well-worn *crescendo* to a **pp** *subito*. Moreover the colours are more clearly differentiated by the 2nd violins' harmonic being now left undoubled by woodwind, and the low woodwind bass line unsupported by double basses. The trumpets are marked down to **pp** and have no hairpins. The revised orchestral setting of this bar is daring and highly original.

pp. 89/91 (138/40)

The omission of the oboe line, an unnecessary extra doubling colour, easily effected by the transferring of its one independent note to the bassoon for the sake of harmonic completeness, greatly enhances the individual quality of the solo violin to whose line a few extra phrase-marks are added to increase the wheedling (*schmeichelnd*) character. Four out of the five triangle strokes have also been suppressed, thus accentuating the importance of the single one remaining.

A new *fliessend* added at the second bar of **57** (**98**) is a well-considered mark after the two *nicht eilen* indications that follow so closely upon one another, the first a bar before, the second a bar after **56** (**98**), pointing the beginning of the *Misterioso* development-cum-episode. For this is the first and more extended of the two dramatic corners at which the flow is held up; but with the change to the tonality of A the progress of the movement must be resumed in anticipation of the principal episodic motif which returns at the third bar of **58** (**99**). This tempo revision is thus essential for the appreciation of the design as a whole and needs to be interpreted with scrupulous precision and understanding.

pp. 92/4 (141/3)

Fig. **59** (**100**) marks the second cornerstone heralding the great surging climactic section of the movement and Mahler adds extra injunctions (*Fliessend . . . etwas drängend*) to urge the music ever forwards.

The change in the upper flute line in the second bar of p. 92 (141) is a clear correction of a misprint, though possibly reflecting an interesting early stage in the composition, elsewhere improved but here forgotten. The faulty alignment of the bass tuba and timpani in the first bar of p. 93 (142) remains uncorrected in all editions, but in the last bar of p. 94 (143) K2 takes the opportunity of restoring the missing sharp to the A of the melodic instruments. K2 also brings the cowbells into line with the rest of the notation by putting their part onto the 'C' space instead of a fourth lower as given in the previous bars. It seems hardly likely that Mahler intended this apparent change of note to carry any significance.

At **60** (**101**) the two-bar bass drum roll is removed (it was certainly quite unnecessary), and the 3rd and 4th oboes instead of adding extra volume to the melody line are pressed into much-needed service with the counterpoint. For this purpose Mahler even bids them take up a pair of richer (but stone-cold) cors anglais – forgotten in the *Orchesterbesetzung* of K2 but included in Ratz – even though technically the notes required are actually within the compass of the oboe. But after two bars they stop abruptly at the end of the page, for there is no sign of any cor anglais overleaf; nor is there the appropriate instruction to resume 3rd and 4th oboes for the next entry three bars before **61** (**102**). It seems more than likely that on turning the page Mahler forgot to carry out his intention, which could have been for them to play at least one further bar – thus using the lower notes and justifying the change of instruments.

pp. 95/9
(144/8)

It is not often that one hears a wholehearted rendering of Mahler's exaggerated expression through the rapidly alternating ebb and flow of tempo, though this is another innovation eagerly adopted by Alban Berg in *Wozzeck* and the *Drei Orchesterstücke*, Op. 6. The violence of the emotion should carry the tempo to a considerable pace as shown by yet further injunctions like those on pp. 93/4 (142/3) but which, added to the *nicht schleppen* already present at **61** (**102**), indicate an almost feverish intensity in a passage that could otherwise easily have been allowed to flag too soon.

And when at last the passion does begin to fade, Mahler saw that the snap of the trombones' *fp* would now strike too sharp a note. So he excised the sforzando at the entry six bars after **62** (**103**), thereby instead allowing the trombone tone to add warmth to the beauty of the wistful closing bars.

The conductor is instructed at the beginning of p. 99 (148) to leave plenty of time for the exceedingly beautiful but treacherous violin phrase, and the celesta marking is reversed to *nicht arpegg.*, two very important revisions to be found in K2. The celesta change is also noted by Redlich in Eul. and certainly it is a most subtle improvement.

III

pp. 100/1
(77/8) The Scherzo once more shows some careful rethinking, suggesting that Mahler considered the character of the movement to have been understressed and the contrasts insufficiently realized.

No one would imagine, glancing at the first page in K1, that the demoniac principal theme given *ff* to all the violins in unison would have seemed to its creator underscored, nor for that matter the subsidiary motif given to four horns and violas. But dissatisfied he was, arguably because with the violins ranged on either side of the rostrum, as was his practice, there was neither enough accumulation of savage weight nor differentiation with the violas who made little impact even with the horn reinforcement, and were in any case undermarked at a single *f*. In consequence, the 2nd violins and violas were interchanged, the countertheme not only being marked up to *ff* but doubled on cellos as well as horns. As for the pounding A's that had occupied the cellos together with basses and timpani, these were no problem and could safely be left to timpani and basses alone, the latter dividing in order to supply the upper octave relinquished by the cellos.

At **63** (**46**) the setting compared too unfavourably with the return of the same music four bars before **70** (**53**). So the lower woodwind reinforcement is taken away from bass trombone and tuba and given to cellos and basses. But Mahler seems to have forgotten that in the later passage the strings complete the figure, instead of stopping one note short (as did the brass in order to prepare for the new figure at the third bar). Perhaps the missing demisemiquaver D sharp should be restored to the cellos and basses.

The removal of many doubling instruments sharpens the lines without any loss of intensity: the bass drum at **63** (**46**), the violas – whose reinforcement of woodwind and trombones served no purpose – the tuba's thicker tone doing more harm than good to the cutting edge of the trombones, themselves now reduced from *ff* to *f*. So the alternating horn quartets are reduced to pairs. Furthermore, lower woodwind make better bed-fellows with the trombones than triply-divided cellos in the two bars before **64 (47)**.

pp.102/4
(79/81)
The sacrifice of the tuba and the diminuendo to a welcome *p* in the first bars of **64 (47)**, together with the removal of the horns and basses in the third and fourth bars, add to the clarity of the cellos' and basses' upward swoops, as well as giving extra point to the basses' re-entry a bar later.

By removing the trumpets at **65 (48)** the undulating motif becomes more specifically the province of the horns, who now play open instead of muted. Moreover, by doing away with the thumps on bass trombone and tuba, those of the percussion are thrown into sharper relief. Mahler's decision to strike out an instrument always has a positive purpose. Hence, too, the pruning of the violas during the three bars after **65 (48)**, which renders proportionately more dramatic the terse phrases left to them. The revised dynamic markings of the lower horns and basses seem logical, though it remains curious that the bass clarinet and contrabassoon were not similarly rethought. The isolated *f* for bass clarinet at the second bar of **65 (48)** is particularly odd. (Perhaps *sf* was meant but that might have presupposed balancing sforzandi in the later phrases to correspond with the contrabassoon.)

The reduction of the timpani/viola entry at the second bar of **66 (49)** to *p* is in line with the general treatment of this section, being dynamically contrasted with the savage opening despite the recurring sudden brief bursts of *ff*. Such *piano* sections accentuate the close similarity of this movement to the Scherzo of Dohnanyi's F sharp minor Suite, Op.19, which, composed five years later, must surely have been written under the direct influence of Mahler's epoch-making work.

pp.105/7
(82/4)
Three bars before **67 (50)** K2 supplies the *offen* to 1st and 2nd horns, whose omission in K1 can only have been an oversight.

But **67** (**50**) itself is completely changed from *ff* to *p* so that the *crescendo* approach now leads to an abrupt drop in dynamics. The woodwind are reduced not only in degree but in thickness and doublings, the oboes especially being greatly simplified. At **68** (**51**) the outbursts of *ff* still stand but these too are less violent, the horns being marked down to a single *f* for the first four bars, and the timpani sacrificed. This allows for greater variety of effect during the succeeding bars where *ff* does apply briefly to the horns (though the full complement are held in reserve until **69** (**52**)) and the timpani entry is the more effective for having been deferred.

A particularly amusing revision is the addition of an exclamation mark in K2 to the *Nicht eilen* that is already present in K1. Mahler clearly did not trust either himself or any other conductor to hold the reins tightly enough without this additional cautionary stroke.

pp.108/10
(85/7)

The removal of the timpani and trumpets in the eighth and ninth bars after **69** (**52**), as of the tuba two bars later, gives a welcome lightening of the texture; while the sprinkling of diminuendi and *piano*s at **70** (**53**) serves to bring the vehemence of the sforzandi into sharper relief.

The omission of the trombones between **70** (**53**) and the third bar of **71** (**54**) makes their sinister entry five bars before **72** (**55**) all the more telling and only necessitates a minor redistribution and re-marking (upwards to *ff* this time) of the horns at **71** (**54**).

But the menacing undulating figure preceding the climax at **72** (**55**) undergoes a wholesale revision of dynamics. The diminuendo in the double basses is now shared by all the lower strings, while the woodwind and brass on the contrary are allowed officially to enjoy the crescendi towards the sforzandi that Mahler may well have found automatically creeping in during the course of rehearsals. (The tuba lacks a *sf* in the fourth bar of **71** (**54**), an omission already present in K1 and never corrected in subsequent versions.)

The climax itself palpably needs some degree of abandon and Mahler in the light of experience added the indication *Flottes Tempo*. 'Flott' was a favourite term of Mahler's at this time, though hardly to be found in the scores of any other composer. 'Jaunty' is perhaps the nearest English equivalent, although this suggests more good humour than is reflected in the present savagely ironical context. The addition of *mf* to the bass-drum line (previously unmarked) was a wise precaution, thus allowing greater prominence to be given to the higher-pitch colours such as the trumpets featuring the ominous major-minor Fate motto, here reappearing after a long absence.

p.111
(88)

The new precipitation of tempo needs checking before the *poco rit.* of only two bars and so Mahler added a stern *nicht mehr eilen!* (no more hurrying!) a full six bars before the change of mood and tempo of **73 (56)**. The dynamic marks of the pizzicato strings are more carefully graded than they had been, and the missing $\Longrightarrow$ *p* is restored to the 2nd trumpet during the second and third bars of the page. This must have been another oversight.

p.112
(89)

Only Mahler, the conductor-composer, who cared so passionately that his message should not be misunderstood, would have added a lengthy note explaining in detail what the commas in the oboe solo are meant to convey – 'little, but not exaggerated breaths'. This is much what one might surely have expected; yet he found it necessary to labour the point, thereby perhaps giving some insight into the difficulties he himself experienced with the Viennese orchestral players of the time. On the other hand, Gerald Abraham in the New Oxford History of Music (Vol.IX, p.6) finds these elaborate instructions indicative of Mahler's insecurity as an orchestral composer, though this is at the very least a controversial view.

A new *nicht eilen* (don't hurry) emphasizes the deliberate tempo of this trio-like 'old-fashioned' (*Altväterisch*) section. It is easy to feel that one is overdoing the stylisation of its curious gait (a problem it shares with the second subject of the Finale of No.7) and the admonition provides welcome corroboration.

At **74 (57)** the interruption clearly lacked sufficient vehemence, for Mahler stepped up both orchestration and dynamics, adding a general comma before the movement resumes its grotesque strut. Mahler may have come to realise that this breath-mark could be misunderstood, for he further added an asterisk that appears to refer the reader again to the note about the earlier commas in the oboe part – although the context is entirely different. Composers' commas are a specialist subject on their own (see also the note on p.106).

pp.113/4 (90/1)

The addition of *Altväterisch* at the top of p.113 (90) instead of at the beginning of the following page, its replacement by a *rit.* on p.114 (91) with a *Wieder wie zuvor* (=*ancora come prima*) two bars later, followed immediately by another new *Nicht eilen* all seem to verge on the fanatical. And yet these very marks and alterations, if honestly observed, make it hardly possible to mis-interpret Mahler's vision, eccentric – even crazy – as it must have seemed to its first audiences and players in 1906. For within its own ethic it is logical and consistent, even including the exaggerations.

The stepping-up of the *f* clarinet three bars before **77** (**60**) to a couple of *ff* players with their bells up in the air is another characteristic touch, though the omission of the extra player at the new system one bar before **77** (**60**) looks very much like a slip.

pp.115/17 (92/4)

The tempo-changes here are more influential on a conductor's interpretation than may appear at a super-ficial glance. For just as the addition of yet another *Nicht eilen* at the second system of p.115 (92) actually means that the music should in fact be held back, so conversely the addition of the exclamation mark to the *nicht schleppen* – the only correction to p.116 (93) – implies even more forward movement than the mere warning not to drag had previously implied. This interpretation is strengthened by the new *Etwas drängend* at the beginning of p.117 (94) which gives a dramatic suggestion of precipitous flight to the repetitions of the little figure:

pp.117/18 (94/5)

As often in Mahler's scherzos, the trio section is composite and embodies a much slower and heavily satirical Ländler. The success of such complicated schemes relies on the transitions being unmistakable and accordingly the ten bars between **80** and **81** (**63** and

103

64) are crucial. Despite the restraining influence of the heavy horn acciaccaturas, Mahler felt it necessary to add *molto tenuto* to all eight horns whilst at the same time intensifying the *pesante* of the last bars to *molto pesante*.

pp.118/20
(95/7)

The entry of the slow Ländler is now itself refined instrumentally. With the lead-in bars cut down and marked back to ***ppp***, the up-beat figure is made starker with simpler means. In K1 it is given to a massed unison of oboes and clarinets but with disparity of phrasings, some playing *p cresc.* and others *ff*. This characteristic device – so telling on paper – here made too confusing an effect and Mahler jettisoned it by cutting out the *ff* players altogether. He then reversed the phrasing of the others to *f* ——— reinforcing them unexpectedly with 1st violins who have to scramble to change to the *col legno* that still stands in the following bar.

The ruthless erasure of the brass ensemble in the first two bars of **81** (**64**) also means that their entry six bars later alternates with that of the horns and bassoons, a far more arresting use of the contrasting timbres.

pp.121/2
(98/9)

Fig. **82** (**65**) marks the abrupt return to the Scherzo proper and hence the beginning of the second time round, so to speak. On p.122 (99), three bars before **83** (**66**), the horns originally had the opposite phrasing to the trombones with whom they were in unison (i.e. *f* === *p* instead of *p* === *f*) but, as at **81** (**64**), the effects must have cancelled each other out for Mahler now brings them into line.

pp.122/9
(99/106)

The changes in the pages that follow reveal an interpretative rethinking of this section of the movement, even though the basic composition remains unaltered.

In the first place the music of p.123 (100) is brought right back to *piano*, although all the sforzandi remain. This is achieved by a general diminuendo hairpin in the first bar of the page, as well as by the total excision of the tuba part already from the last bar of the previous page. Some inconsistency of dynamics will be noticed here but the obtrusive and biting fortissimo of the xylophone creates a startling effect against the strings' *p* that must certainly have been intentional; and by the first bar of p.124 (101) the strings themselves have now risen briefly to *ff* only to collapse again in the following bar. At **84** (**67**) the 1st violins are also far more dramatic with their new *mf*'s punctuated by the savage *ff* interjections.

Moreover the tam-tam, together with the pizzicato cellos (though not, strangely enough, the timpani), now join the harps' reiterations already at the beginning of the *Etwas zurückhaltend* instead of a bar later.

This passage is additonally marked *ritenuto*, the first of a succession of tempo-changes over the next few pages. The sinister undulation of this motif needs more spacious treatment to achieve its effect and on its return towards the end of the movement (p.144 (121)) the *ritenuto* is again added. At this slower pace the expressive character of the one-bar after-phrase is enhanced by the little extra *p* ⟨ indications.

The pull back of tempo is continued still further with a *langsamer* on p.125 (102), the effect of which is that this whole section is kept at a more moderate tempo, acquiring a character of its own instead of merely falling into place as an elaborated reprise of the Scherzo. In contrast, however, the *Flott* of the linking bars is not only retained but persists, this time during the whole nine bars of p.128 (105), the *nicht eilen* having been removed. Instead, an abrupt *ritenuto* pulls up the headlong rush barely in time for the return of the Trio at the beginning of p.129 (106).

pp.129/32
(106/9)

Once again Mahler seems to be obsessed by the fear that conductors will not credit just how steadily he means the music to go (*poco meno mosso* is changed to *Merklich langsamer* – noticeably slower – followed by two *Nicht eilen*s in rapid succession). Isolated bars are also subjected to interesting changes of colour: the third and fifth bars after **88** (**71**) show a flute *added* (the additions are very few compared with the excisions) to the oboe solo, giving a mixed timbre to just these isolated phrases. The 1st horn is also added to one of the oboes' and violins' bars of figuration at **90** (**73**), though significantly not to both. (To have continued into the next bar would have obscured the change of timbre as the brass take over the pattern so dramatically.) On the other hand, the strings are thinned out between the fifth and eighth bars after **90 (73)** and the timpani loses a phrase which, though striking and effective, detracted from its more important motivic entry two bars later at **91 (74)**.

p.133
(110)

Not only is the cymbal stroke removed but a *rit.* added to the $\frac{2}{8}$ bar before the comma. This dramatic moment must have come unstuck; certainly Mahler's intention was far less clear before he added an asterisk plus the word *Luftpause* at the top and bottom of the page. Composers vary greatly in their interpretation of a comma, which does not necessarily interrupt the pulse. In Stravinsky, for example, a comma normally has no more effect than to shorten the note immediately preceding it. Moreover, Mahler himself had added a general comma representing only a short breath-mark after the three *drängend* bars at **74 (57)**. One result of spelling out his intentions time after time tends to be that where he does not do so there is far less need to exaggerate. Here the breath is clearly a big one and justifies the pull-up on the violins, as they approach the brink of the precipice.

p.134
(111)

The simultaneous inversion of the 1st violins' phrase, originally a bassoon solo, is now given to no fewer than three bassoons marked up to *f*, an analogous change to that of the strident clarinets at the parallel place in the first Trio (see p.103 above). Against the **pp** strings (the cellos and 2nd violins have their missing **pp**'s added) this should make an equally hilarious effect, which Mahler features by lightening the texture still further – the violas are removed altogether from the two relevant bars – and with the addition of another *nicht eilen!* to enable the bevy of bassoons to make the most of the *keck* (impudent) phrases rearing up to their high G's so grotesquely.

p.135
(112)

The replacement of the trumpets (as background to the massed staccato woodwind) by decisive *sempre ff* pizzicati on the 2nd violins is a well-judged change of colour, being sharper but at the same time more transparent. In the same way, *drängend* makes a more positive instruction than the relatively mild *nicht schleppen*. This time, unlike the analogous place **78 (61)** in the first Trio, Mahler now prescribes a new *rit.* to lead back to the

Wieder wie zu Anfang, which is further graced by yet another *nicht eilen!* three bars later.

pp.136/9
(113/16)

Here is a unique revision of a purely practical nature: the $\frac{3}{4}$ bar at the end of the page is broken up with an extra barline into two $\frac{3}{8}$ bars. Mahler must have found the passage clumsy to conduct and the subtlety of the cross-accent at the repeat of the phrase merely pedantic.

pp.139/40
(116/17)

This passage corresponds with **81** (**64**) and the new mark *fast langsam* (almost slow) is necessary to indicate the tempo relationship of the two sections in a way that the original *Ancora meno mosso* failed to do.

In the first two bars of p.140 (117) the harps have lost two chords. These are the unique pages which call for four harps (see p.68) although there are not even two separate parts. However, far from confirming that the indications '4 Harfen' are an oversight (they could not have escaped Mahler's notice as he worked on this exhaustive labour of love) the revision could on the contrary be taken to show that their retention was deliberate and that Mahler really did have before him the splendid image of the row of shining harps and wanted the sound of all four during this passage, *piano* but significant as the chords are. Where the harps enter at **96** (**79**) they are further emphasized through the cutting-out of the trombones, tuba and cellos, while the bass clarinet and bassoon are marked down to *piano*. Two bars later the trumpet and half the horns are removed, and the remaining horns stop a bar earlier to allow for the bass clarinet solo which is marked up to *forte*. At the third bar of p.140 (117) the horns are now muted.

pp.141/2
(118/19)

Here the change is fundamental, although Mahler can certainly never have played this second vehement return of the Scherzo as shown in K1. For the revision supplies a *Tempo I subito* corresponding with that at **82** (**65**) on p.121 (98). It is ushered in, moreover, by a reinforcement of the muted horns' snarl by the other four players in the bar before **97** (**80**), though with the subtlety that the new entrants have a *diminuendo* hairpin while the original horns (who are playing the very same notes) remain *ff*.

There are also some typically Mahlerian changes of colour. The *ff* string entry now collapses during a single bar – a less neatly dovetailed reading but boldly dramatic. The cellos however no longer take part but after an abrupt bar's rest join the basses in the lower strand of counterpoint, replacing the bass trombone and tuba who are delayed until the beginning of p.142 (119). The basses also rest for a bar instead of doubling the timpani, in order to start the line from the beginning. In making this revision, marked *ff*, the single *f* of the basses' original entry a bar later has been (surely mistakenly) retained in K2 as well as in Ratz.

Where the bass trombone and tuba do enter (now marked up to *f*) the timpani is removed; this seems something of a sacrifice as it had referred motivically to the strings' entry five bars earlier.

pp.143/4
(120/1)

The general *diminuendo* to *piano* across the second and third bars of **98** (**81**) is a new and interesting concept, although the *sfp* marks in woodwind and violas with which it is followed correspond with the changes on p.123 (100). The return to *ff* occurs four bars before **99** (**82**), with an extra *ff* given to each of the woodwind staves at the beginning of p.144 (121). The excision of the bass trombone and tuba across the whole of p.143 (120) also relates to that of the tuba in the earlier context; the parallel addition of *Ritenuto* for the undulating chordal motif after **99** (**82**) has already been discussed (see p.105).

As earlier on, three bars before **83** (**66**), the contrary motion of the horns' dynamics clearly failed to satisfy Mahler and again he brings them into line. It is fascinating, however, that in so doing he does not establish the phrasing of the earlier appearance of the theme (at **84** (**67**) and especially at **65** (**48**), which is the true analogy of context) but chooses the version that is to some degree the opposite of these, and so all the more arresting.

pp.145/8
(122/5)

In K2 the climax of the movement is drawn out with a mark of *Gehalten*, which gives the oboes every opportunity to raise their bells and scream out their caricature of a fanfare. On the other hand the flutes' chromatic scale would have lost its dramatic effect and become merely pedantic at the slower tempo if Mahler had not now directed it to be played flutter-tongued.

At **101** (**84**) the drum beats rise only to *p* instead of *mf* and the unrealistic four-bar diminuendo of the contrabassoon is severely shortened. The strings, who had specifically put on their mutes for the sake of the weird, ghostly climax, take them off again on p.146 (123), which gives a better quality to the solo passages.

A bassoon is added to the ends of the cellos' phrases (i.e. at each $\frac{3}{4}$ bar in the upper system of p.148 (125)), the last held triad of A minor is whittled away by the omission of the bassoons, the trombones also vanishing to *pp*, and the movement ends no longer with the triad itself but with a shocked silence after the timpani solo, lightly reinforced for the sake of clarity by pizzicato double-basses. The whole last page is also made to slow right down to a final *Langsam* for that ominous closing figure.

IV

p.149

For the Finale Mahler draws for the first time on the total resources he has allowed himself for the symphony, including the five-fold woodwind, six trumpets, a fourth trombone, and an immense range of extra percussion including the famous Hammer. Nevertheless, much as in the first movement he had decided to do without the tambourine, so here he did away with the whip (*Holz-klapper*) which is no longer to be found in the list of instruments.

At some time after the completion of the score, Mahler seems further to have contemplated adding to the orchestration of the Finale two extra tubas (possibly Wagner tubas) as well as a tenor-horn, the latter anticipating his actual use of this unusual instrument in the opening of the Seventh Symphony. Although this extra revision was never carried out, it is of great interest and is therefore illustrated in the reproductions of pages from the autograph shown between pp.110 and 113. I am greatly indebted to Donald Mitchell for drawing my attention to these projected revisions.

The Finale is an enormous movement lasting a full half hour. It also begins with a long and introspective slow introduction whose significance is revealed only at

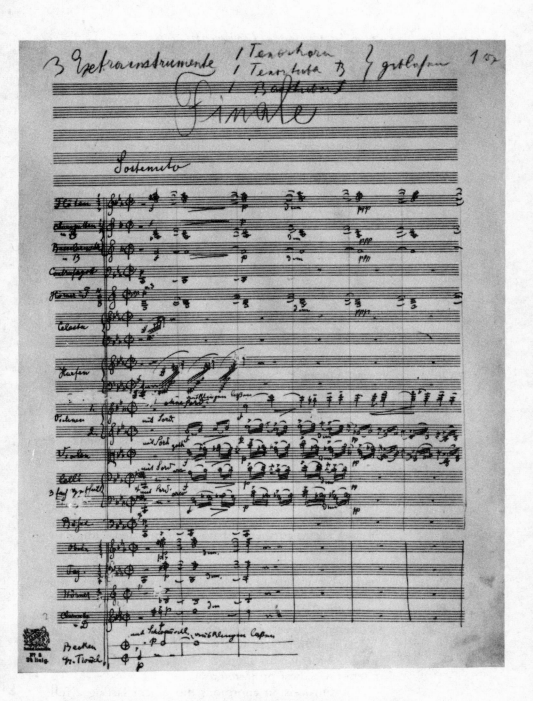

Autograph pages from the Finale of the Sixth Symphony,
showing the projected use of tenor horn and Wagner tubas

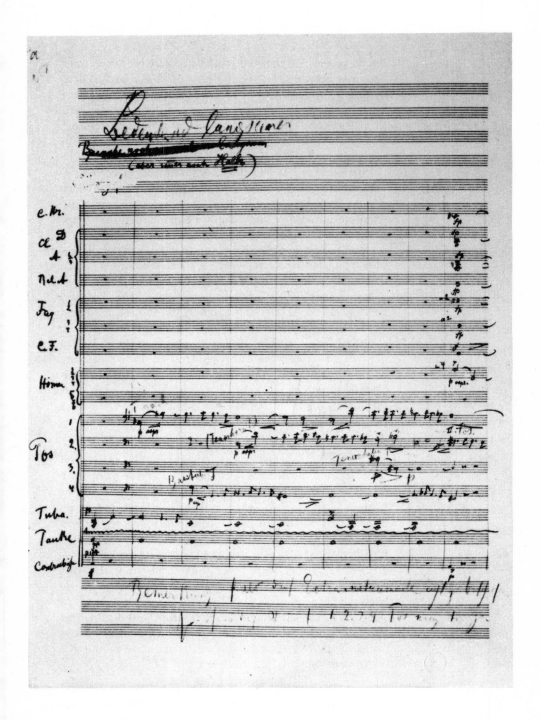

the very end of the symphony. Expansive as it must certainly be, the movement must not be allowed to drag or else its complex and many-sided argument collapses into incoherence. Mahler's change of the tempo indication *Sostenuto* into *Allegro moderato* for the Prefatory section is thus of the utmost importance, since, as transpires at **104**, the tempi are directly related.

Furthermore, there must be no question of a half-hearted beginning, even though the diminished seventh which forms the background to the violins' first impassioned utterance is atmospheric in character. Perhaps Mahler felt frustrated at the first performances on receiving too faint a response when giving the first down beat of the giant movement, which we know meant so much to him in a directly personal way.

So the cellos' pizzicato bottom C, the rustling tremolo of the central strings, and the violins' outburst itself are all marked up to *ff*. The celesta must have sounded feeble and its little arpeggio is now played in octaves – this makes a surprising difference – while the harps are also reinforced by the use of both hands in close formation, playing not simple arpeggios but glissandi which in the case of this particular chord is perfectly practical by means of enharmonic tuning, as Rimsky-Korsakov showed in many a brilliant passage.

p.150   The violins' declamation is additionally reinforced with accents and at the first double-bar they are now joined not only by the other strings but by all eight horns. This is a highly significant moment, for at its ultimate repetition on p.260 (four pages before the end of the symphony) it is the shock moment of the third and fatal hammer blow – but more of this in its proper place. At present it is enough to establish that the Fate motif on the heavy brass drops to *pp* in a single bar, that the harp glissando is given longer to make its effect (bearing in mind the alteration to a quicker tempo, no doubt) and that the great motif of the strings and horns is now punctuated with rests, a recurrent revision in this movement (see p.129 below).

p.151   The steep *diminuendo* added to the bass drum and heavy brass, the commas between the cellos' semi-breves, and the change to *f* of the punctuating basses'

114

pizzicato at **104**, recalling the similar change in the Fifth Symphony at the last bar of the first movement – these are all touches calculated to bring the shape of the music into sharper relief.

From this point of view it is surprising that there is no revision of the dotted motif in tuba and bassoons on this page. Comparison with the analogous horn passages on pp.224/5, as well as similar places on the last page of the symphony, suggests that the need for this exaggerated punctuation in the pursuit of a sharp, clearer texture grew on Mahler as he worked and that he forgot to turn back and bring this first entry into line.

At this point there occurs the first use of a device that Mahler used repeatedly both in the Finale now under discussion and also in later works such as the Seventh Symphony and the *Lied von der Erde*: that is, the unusual instruction for the harp, *Mediator*. The explanation for this is not to be found in any book of instrumentation. It really means a plectrum, although in practice harpists normally use their finger-nails.

p.152   The tuba and 4th horn are marked up to *f* and *mf* respectively. After the rich sounds of four bassoons and bass clarinet, imitations in *p* were apt to sound too tentative.

The listing of 'Tiefes Glockgel.' (=‘-geläute’) on this page has an asterisk against it but there is no corresponding footnote in either K1 or K2. Ratz and Eul. were surely right in adding a reference back to the footnote on the first page of the Finale, p.149. Like the cowbells discussed on pp.77–8 above, this was a new and important effect created by Mahler for the first time in this symphony and adopted by Webern in his two sets of *Orchesterstücke*. Not that this was by any means the first time Mahler had used bells, even bells of indeterminate pitch struck randomly, for these can be found in the exultant closing pages of the Second Symphony. But the idea of 'two or more very deep bells of indefinite but differing pitch placed in the distance and struck softly and irregularly', as described in the footnote of p.149, was certainly new. The cowbells themselves make no appearance here, being reserved for the return of this passage at the beginning of the development (see p.123

below); but the allusion to the pastoral scene that formed the central tableau of the first movement is clearly underlined by the use of similar motivic writing, especially in the shimmering background music.

The deep very distant bells, even more than the off-stage cowbells, create a most delicate effect and are easily covered by the orchestra. Thus although Mahler had from the first taken care to orchestrate over the bells with the utmost economy, he found it necessary to take even further measures to make sure that they would be heard. The pizzicato 2nd violins are removed and the entire clarinet department marked down with a *diminuendo* to **ppp**.

pp.153/4   The changes on these pages are extraordinary and far-reaching. That the wild outbursts surrounding the rearing motif on horns and then trumpets should be part of a prevailingly dragging tempo was far too undramatic for the impatient Mahler. Yet it is a very difficult passage to play. Thus a succession of tempo changes plus extra injunctions seemed the only way of perpetuating what the tormented composer found himself actually doing in practice. A new *più mosso* halfway through the fourth bar after **105** would give the necessary urgency. But the horns had been marked not to hurry – and indeed they were hardly capable of doing any such thing if a passage such as:

was to be played with any degree of accuracy. So the sense of urgency Mahler gave with one hand through his *più mosso* he partially took away with the other by adding *aber nicht eilen* in the general directive, at the same time giving to the horns a helpful *Zeit lassen* ('allow time').

The following bars (the first two on p.154) now bring back the tempo to its dragging gait with a new *Rit . . . wieder schleppend* replacing the earlier *nicht eilen!*, while the awkward and dangerous trumpet fanfare is actually marked *Langsam*. At the third bar of the new page the *più mosso* is once more introduced, this time however without the cautionary postscript. The horns' frenzied diminution of the tuba's motif, itself reinforced by two more horns and marked 'brutal', will allow for no such restraint.

The 1st violins' tremolo at the beginning of the page is delayed by a bar. Even in K1 it was marked down to *ppp* and constituted no more than a doubling of the violas, in the same way as the *pp* tremolo of the flutes reinforces the violins' own line in the following bar. But this now becomes a dramatic *f* entry, a very positive gain in return for so slight a sacrifice.

Of the other orchestral *retouches* the most remarkable is the complete reversal in the use of the harps. Their reinforcement of the harmonies made up by tremolo strings is now abandoned in favour of doubling the jerky bass-figure, though this is not in itself a particularly suitable kind of passage-work for harp sonority in the lower register.

The tuba solo in the last bar of p.154 is marked up to *f* (at the new quicker tempo it can easily be submerged), whereas on the contrary the violas in the same bar are reduced from *f* to match the *p* of the other strings. In fact, despite the *sf* in the clarinets, with whom the violas are in unison, their *f* may very well have been an error, like the omission of the bassoons' diminuendo hairpin, now restored.

pp.155/6   By taking out the horns and tuba from the first three bars of the heavy chorale-like wind section, a far better change of colour is effected when they replace the clarinets four bars later. At **107** the harp glissando preparation for this structural cornerstone of the movement is extended to occupy two beats instead of one (a revision that Mahler repeats in the last bar of p.159), and the trumpets are marked *offen* for the formal enunciation of the major-minor triad motto. This must always have been Mahler's intention, although the indication was missing in K1. These strident entries of the motto themes at key points of the design are at first all on open brass as in the first movement, the muted snarl only being added to intensify the threat of these themes from the recapitulation onwards.

pp.157/9   Between the third and eighth bars after **107** Mahler made a subtle change of emphasis rarely brought out in performance. He removed the accents from the lowest horn line (i.e. the 4th and 8th players), leaving the necessary stresses to the already accented tremolo strings; but at the repeat of the phrase two bars later he allowed the horn accents to remain, because here it is the strings who are unaccented and the responsibility thus passes to the horns. He did, however, add one single *sfp* accent to the strings at the moment of climax in the wind motif, followed by a *dim.* to *pp* two bars later. The imitation in oboes and clarinets is also brought into sharper relief by making both horns finish together, only the bassoon sustaining the end note of the phrase.

At **108** the 4th bassoon is added to the other three in a general unison of the bass line. This is more perhaps for the satisfaction of the player than for any detectable difference in the audible effect. The *sf* in the 1st and 2nd horns in place of the diminuendo (still, however, to be found in the cor anglais who plays with them) is an interesting new touch, as are the changes of attack in the 1st oboe and upper line of cellos who share the new entry on the last bar of p.158.

pp.160/1   Here we reach the beginning of the principal Allegro section whose importance must not be allowed to escape the listener. Accordingly Mahler strengthened every string entry of the jerky principal subject, each section in turn being marked up either to *f* (in cellos – more was not necessary as there are already no less than four bassoons playing *ff* in unison) or to *ff* (in violins and violas). The horns and trumpets are also slightly adjusted and the 3rd horn removed from its doubling of the 1st (who is marked *offen* though it is difficult to see why, since he is already open).

p.162   The last bars of the build-up to the Allegro are certainly simpler and thus more directly effective in the revised version, but at the sacrifice of one of Mahler's most imaginative tricks of unconventional instrumentation, that of making half a section – in this instance the trumpets – play in unison with the other half, but in a crescendo against a sustained *ff* of their colleagues. Mahler introduced this splendidly ingenious idea with eight horns into his edition of Beethoven's Ninth Symphony, to enhance the great build-up of the 'An die

Freude' melody. Here he had already tried to use it in
the Scherzo, though only in a short upbeat phrase, but
had thrown it out in K2 (see p.104 above); and now
once more he decided against it and even added hand-
stopped horns to augment the uniformly snarling
crescendo of the muted trumpets.

p.163

The horns are again open at the arrival of the *Allegro
energico,* but the 7th and 8th are dropped from the first
phrase in order that they may be reintroduced with
stronger, fresher effect at the up-beat to the third bar.
The 1st trumpet is also now unmuted and remains so
until the bar before **112** (the exact opposite to the
original). Down-bows are added to the two minims in
all strings at the bar of **110**, as also again at the parallel
places on pp.164/5 and after.

pp.164/6

The earlier cutting off of the clarinets, bassoons, cellos
and basses, the decrescendo of the side drum in place of
the abrupt *fp* – though followed by alternate *p*'s and
mf's so as to emphasize only the more important of its
rhythms – and the omission of cellos and basses for the
two bars at **111**, all unite in focusing the drama on the
timpani; similarly the suppression of the trombones at
the third bar of **111** pinpoints the slashes of colour of
the lower string chords, now augmented by the violas
and an extra note on the cellos.

Some thinning has also been carried out – two horns
in place of four in the second and third bars after **111**
(curious that in making this revision the missing crotchet
rest was not noticed and restored); the 3rd and 4th
trumpets no longer double the woodwind except for the
last rising phrase that is made more striking as a result;
the 5th and 6th trumpets' doubling of the sustained D
in lower horns must have totally obscured the violas and
cellos for it is also removed together with further
doublings on the violas and timpani, all sacrificed in the
justifiable fear of over-emphasis.

But the trumpets' muting shows a positive change. In
the original score trumpets 1 and 3 were specifically
unmuted at the bar before **112** even though the others
remained muted. This confusing mixture of timbres is
ironed out in the revision, all the trumpets being muted
and making their entry together in the one bar before

112. The now necessary indication for the 1st and 2nd players to unmute before the solo three-trumpet entry on p.166 is omitted by K2 but rightly restored by Ratz. This entry was originally, and strangely, scored for the 1st, 2nd and 5th players. This cannot have been good for ensemble and Mahler substituted the obvious No.3 player for No.5, who, however, retains his muted solo during the four bars before **114**.

The percussion is once more severely reduced. The loss of the cymbal stroke in the bar before **112** is unexpected but wise; there is a dangerous profusion in this finale. So too the side drums and cymbal rolls three and five bars before **113** have vanished.

pp.167/71   During the five bars after **113** Mahler had created the strange effect of the bassoons and bass clarinet emerging at brief intervals from the vehemence of the cellos and basses, with whom they play in unison. But the short diminuendi during the sustained A's in the third and fifth bars proved altogether insufficient for so subtle a detail and Mahler replaced them with earlier hairpins dropping right back to *p*. Strangely, however, the hairpins and *p*'s come in different places, making a new and remarkable variation of phrasing between the two closely similar passages. (The missing accents in horns 5–8 during the third and fourth bars after **113** were duly noticed during the revision and restored. Redlich failed to spot that point in Eul.)

Three bars before **115** the horn writing proved oversophisticated and Mahler simplified the lines by adding the 3rd and 4th horns to the 5th and 7th already at the beginning of the phrase and bringing their dynamics into line. Incongruously enough, only the single *f* in 3rd and 4th one bar before **115** has remained. Originally it had been the climax of a crescendo from *p*. Now it should certainly be changed to *ff*.

Five bars before **116** the bass drum roll had originally no dynamic at all. This Mahler now marked *p* ◁────── though still without specifying how far the crescendo should go.

pp.172/4   The maelstrom descent to the second subject is thoroughly revised, for the original was not only overscored and over-marked with repeated sforzandi and fortissimos until nearly the last bar before **117** (where the new motif in its bright new colours and tonality suddenly shines out), but the tempo was held back by the overall *pesante* indication in the middle of p.173. Instead, the new injunction *nicht schleppen* – (= don't drag) already appears at the second bar of the same page. This not only enhances the wildness of the passage, but leads more naturally into the *fliessend* of the *sempre l'istesso tempo* at **117**.

The Holzklapper (whip) is removed altogether (as was already foreseen on p.109 above in connection with the list of instruments on the first page of the movement). The cymbal roll in bar 2 of p.173 has also vanished. The woodwind semiquaver doubling of the rushing strings is curtailed at the third bar of p.172 and the horns and brass are substantially reduced.

The *diminuendo* in the bars before **117** is now carefully graded, together with an ingeniously alternate use of the eight horns. The timpani and cellos are both deleted one bar before **117**, exposing the pizzicato basses as well as preparing for the cellos' own pizzicato chord at the bar-line of the new section, now marked up to *mf*.

One or two loose ends have been tidied up by Ratz. The 5th horn tie left hanging in mid-air in K2 (four bars before **117**), as a result of thinning out in revision, has been removed; and the misprinted timpani dynamic is corrected two bars before **117** (it should read the same as in the previous bar).

pp.177/9   After two pages with no alterations, the next change comes as something of a shock: at the fourth bar of p.177 the *ff* timpani note is now marked for cymbals. Possibly the original had been a slip – certainly the isolated timpani D capping the bass drum crescendo was far less effective than the splendour of a cymbal clash. Yet, in making the change, the printers, whilst retaining the stave with its bass clef for the cymbals (elsewhere notated on a single line) curiously took the trouble of moving the note-head a line upwards to F.

The other major alteration is the distribution of the string lines in bars 4/5 of p.177. Not only do the 2nd violins now jump up to join the 1sts in these bars, but each bar is marked by double- or treble-stopped acciaccaturas to emphasize the new vehement sforzandi. The whole purpose of these bars has in fact become vastly accentuated. As for the original line of the 2nd violins, this is now taken over by the violas, who climb sky-high for the single bar six after **118** and then jump down the octave to join the horns in the two following bars.

Similar changes to the violins continue during the four bars before **119**, acciaccaturas and all. The trombones are, on the other hand, thinned out during these bars, even though this meant substituting increased horn tone in the last two bars before the *Belebend*.

On p.179 Mahler took the opportunity of correcting a serious, if understandable, printer's error in 1st and 2nd trumpets. So similar is the bar in question (three after **119**) to the preceding bar in 3rd and 4th trumpets that the engraver made them actually identical, over-looking the fact of the shorter note-value in the middle of the bar:

In K2 Mahler emphasized the point not only by making the engraver spread the quaver figure in the second of the above bars and remove the triplet '3' sign, but by insisting on the insertion of a footnote:

N.B. ♩♪♪♩ ist keine Triole.

(though in so doing he forgot the F sharp). This so captivated Redlich in Eul. that he discussed it in his Critical Commentary and further reproduced the whole page of K2 in facsimile. By contrast, Ratz made the incredible decision to cut out the splendid and all-important footnote altogether.

pp.180/1

On p.180 the horn and trumpet parts are lightened and clarified whilst at **120** the cymbals are cut out. Even the bass drum roll is now quickly dropped in intensity to *p*. There is an interesting point here, for this is the first cornerstone of the giant movement, a crucial moment that might well have been selected for one of the famous hammer blows. On the contrary, Mahler chose to reduce even such punctuation as he had first given it. His purpose, however, becomes clear if one examines the overall structure of the movement: the returns of the opening bar at **120**, **143** and **164** are not the moments of greatest percussive emphasis, even though the bass notes always require the utmost weight. In this respect a cymbal clash is in any case the wrong colour – a deep sound is needed, as supplied by the bass drum. This is therefore retained but with a diminuendo to **p** added, bringing it into line with the other bass instruments.

pp.181/4   These pages contain the first bars of the long and diffuse development section, that begins like the Finale's slow opening. The violins' soaring theme is, however, inverted and quickly subsides into a corresponding reminiscence of the pastoral music from the development of the first movement, though this time complete with the cowbells in addition to the deep bells of the Finale itself.

Two bars before **121** the *Rit.* is spelt out in full as *Ritenuto*. This looks at first glance as if Mahler was being intolerably pernickety, but it raises an important issue, i.e. the difference between *Rit.* and *Rall.* Normally *ritenuto* means 'held back' – that is to say, at a uniform rate – while *rallentando* signifies a progressive slowing down. But *rit.* could equally be the abbreviation for *ritardando* which is also a gradual process, and it is not by any means always obvious which is meant when the simple *rit.* appears in the score. Often only the musical sense can be the guide to the best interpretation and there are many instances where a choice has to be made purely on artistic judgement. Here *ritardando* might have been perfectly possible and Mahler was at pains to clarify the matter since it was a step-by-step and not a progressive change of pulse that he wanted.

He also inserted the time-signatures ($\frac{4}{4}$ and $\frac{2}{2}$) at **121** and the fourth bar after **121** respectively, even though the bracketed indications *Viertel* and *Langsame Halbe* already stood against the tempo markings.

Where instrumentation is concerned, the tuba is again marked up, as on p.152, though here to *mf*. It is a soft-grained instrument for all its potential weight of tone, and quiet as the passage is, a solo of this importance would not tell sufficiently in *piano*. The 1st harp harmonics are marked up to *f* at the fourth bar of **121** but drop out for the last two bars of p.182 together with the flutes who have, moreover, already stopped the minim pulsation two bars earlier. On the other hand, the harp's *f* minims reappear by themselves for the first three bars of p.183, which suggests a probable oversight on Mahler's part, especially in view of the new *diminuendo* hairpin in the celesta.

The trumpet and trombone solos on p.183 are now muted, a typically Mahlerian revision (cf. the Finale of the First Symphony, fig.27), and the background woodwind chording is removed for four bars, making more sense of their entry with the augmented imitation.

Lastly in this section the string interjections are made more vivid, the 2nd violins' double-stop pizzicato at **122** being stepped up to *f* (the effect of the double-stop on a unison having hardly enough intensity in *piano* to justify itself) and the cellos' reminiscences of the jerky principal subject are raised to *ff*. A single *f* without basses – and Mahler makes a special point at the beginning of the line on p.184 that they *are* without basses – was too pale to alternate on a comparable scale with the rearing phrases of the massed lower woodwind. When on p.185 the basses join in, Mahler leaves the dynamic at the original *f*.

p.185/9   At **123**, as at **117** with which this passage corresponds, the harp chord that marks the change of mood and colour is reinforced. In the earlier passage there was already a pizzicato cello chord that was simply strengthened. Here there was nothing of the kind and Mahler introduced a new pizzicato chord on violas and cellos, marked *ff* and *f* respectively.

The trumpet call which begins on the fifth bar of p.186 is reduced to a mysterious *pp*, whereas the soaring 1st flute is given a rise and fall. Two horns are now ample strengthening to the cellos' and bassoons' swooping phrases during the five bars before **124**. The answering swoops on 2nd violins and woodwind are also cut back, the oboes being dropped altogether and the violins' glissandi simplified to a unison on the topmost notes of the chords.

But from the bar before **124** the differences reflect Mahler's total dissatisfaction. The elaborate orchestral polyphony, magnificent and exciting as it looks on paper, must have sounded confusing and have failed to convey the musical thinking behind so much vehemence. In the first place the speed of events is reduced, partly by the overall substitution of *sostenuto* for *immer dasselbe Tempo* at **124**, and by the spreading out of the up-beat in upper strings from triplet semiquavers to triplet quavers which accordingly start a whole beat earlier. The effect is more far-reaching than it seems; a new breadth of pace is thereby set in motion in which emphasis is no longer swamped by pandemonium. Sustaining woodwind parts are to an overriding extent given the main thematic interest in broad unisons, whether in treble (together with upper strings) or bass (doubling the previously underscored cellos and double basses). The complicated rushing around of the middle strings is replaced by straightforward bold reinforcements of the principal thematic lines. (In fact the surviving 2nd violin semiquavers two bars before **125** look like an oversight that slipped through the net. Should the 2nd violins not play in unison with the 1sts as they now do in the bars on either side, one wonders?) The violas, in particular, are completely rewritten over nine consecutive bars, so as to remove all independence of movement in favour of doublings whether of violins, woodwind, cellos or, in the bar of **125**, horns.

Such violin elaborations as survive are also simplified by the removal of double-strokes in the groups of five ascending quavers. Mahler also took the opportunity to adjust what must surely have been a rhythmic error in the 1st violins four bars before **125**. Dynamics generally are rethought, in particular those of the solo 1st trumpet which are now hardly less than spectacular. Timpani rolls are cut back to a minimum, and – an intriguing detail – the harp chords that precede their huge sweeping glissandi are reconstituted, no doubt on the advice of Mahler's harpists at the first performances.

The first two bars of p.189 have a distinctly odd look apart from the 2nd violin passage already mentioned. The abrupt cessation of the oboes at the beginning of the page, of the clarinets in mid-flight in the middle of the bar, the equally abrupt re-appearance of the pedal A in lower woodwind (in the original it had been sustained through the preceding bars), all seem to point to something left incomplete or at least some alterations not fully carried out. Indeed one whole melodic strand has got lost in the process. Yet there is no possibility of reconstruction and one must play the passage as Mahler left it.

pp.189/91   At **125** the horns and oboes, the latter re-entering most effectively after the brief new respite, begin a swell from **p**. Two extra oboes then join the countertheme at the upper octave in **ff** to replace the 2nd violins who are playing in unison with the 1sts, though in typical Mahlerian style their dynamics or bowings are not always the same. On p.190 the trumpets and cymbal thickenings five and four bars before **126** have disappeared, as have the horn trills two bars later, the 1st trumpet being marked up to *f*. In fact the trumpet is now the primary and not merely a supporting colour.

Page 191 is largely unaltered except for two small touches. The oboes, unlike the other instruments with whom they were in unison, had been allowed to finish their phrase at **127**. This was purposeless and in K2 their concluding crotchet A is no longer to be seen. More curious still is the change in the line for horns 2 and 4 who now hold their D natural on the last bar of the page for a full semibreve. Although superficially the movement of the horns in sixths seems an attractive idea, the fact that the lower line formed an unreal unison with the leaping ninth of the bass line must have clouded the stark counterpoint.

pp.192/4   These pages contain the build-up to the first cornerstone of this tripartite development. In the third bar of p.192 the passionate entry of the 2nd violins and violas is reinforced by two oboes. Marked only a single *f*, these hardly make a substantial difference, though the extra cutting edge of their tone should not be underrated. The addition of clarinets in a to-and-fro handling of what had been a consistent oboe passage in bars 5/7 of the same page, as well as the addition of the fat, soft tone of four flutes to the penetrating quality of three unison horns in their upper register, are all the luxuries of an imaginative and skilled orchestrator rather than the urgent necessities of a frustrated composer whose message has failed to communicate. Nevertheless they are indications of what to Mahler were the important features to be accentuated in rehearsal. Equally, the newly insistent *ff* phrases of the D clarinet underline the *unaccented* pair of descending crotchets in oboes, clarinets and 2nd violins five and four bars before **128**, and in the second bar of p.133 the flutes suddenly jump up to join the upper melodic line. Mahler failed to spot the missing slur in the 1st clarinet four bars before **128** and this is uncorrected even in Ratz.

The 1st violins rest in the bar before **128** in preparation for their new entry (the violas cover their retreat instead of doubling the 2nds), and the three trumpets who double the horns' and bassoons' accented minims are reduced to two. This is in order that the freed trumpet (the second player) can then be given a new assignment during the last two bars of the page during which he gently (*mf*) reinforces the *ff* 1st horn but without continuing into the last bars before **129**, since the doubling is already given to the 3rd and 4th trumpets, though these are now instructed to play 'Bells up'.

p.194   At **129** we reach the first of the hammer blows for which this symphony is notorious. Few orchestral effects have caused so much heart-searching and experimental research as this formidable concept. Mahler's *idea* is clear enough; Alma Mahler has written in detail of the composer's autobiographical, partly prophetic, vision of the 'three blows of fate'. Both Schönberg and Berg adopted this new orchestral device (in *Die Glückliche Hand* and the *Drei Orchesterstücke*, Op. 6 respectively) but without in any way clarifying the outstanding issue: how exactly is the hammer blow to be accomplished? The actual sound Mahler wanted is described in some detail in a footnote to p.194 of the score as 'short, mighty but dull in resonance, with a *non*-metallic character', though in K2 he added the further suggestion 'wie ein Axthieb' – i.e.

like the stroke of an axe. Above all it should be over-whelming. Erwin Stein, when once asked for his opinion, expressed the belief that what should be struck by the great hammer must be 'some kind of membrane' and this would seem to be borne out by Alma's narrative which, although not explicitly concerned with the hammer blows, only makes sense if interpreted in relation to them:

> Mahler had a reading rehearsal of his Sixth Sym-phony with the Philharmonic in the spring. The notes of the bass drum in the last movement were not loud enough for him; so he had an enormous chest made and stretched with hide. It was to be beaten with clubs. He had this engine brought in before the re-hearsal. The members of the orchestra crowded round the monster on the lighted stage – the rest of the house was in darkness. There was the breathless silence of suspense. The drummer raised his arm and smote: the answer was a dull, subdued boom. Once more – with all his strength: the result was the same. Mahler lost patience. Siezing the bludgeon from the man's hand he whirled it aloft and brought it down with a mighty whack. The answering boom was no louder than before. Everyone laughed. And now they brought out the old bass drum again – and the true thunder came. Nevertheless, Mahler had his chest dispatched at great cost to Essen, where it was again tried out, and finally rejected as unfit for service.[1]

However, in reality no membrane can ever simulate Mahler's axe-like thud, and furthermore few thuds will compete with the weight and sheer volume of orchestral drums. In the revised score Mahler found it necessary to add a *ff* bass drum stroke at this first all-important hammer blow, but this accentuates rather than solves the difficulty. For the necessity of finding some sound which differs from that of the bass drum, and to which the latter provides no more than an extra reinforcement, becomes pre-eminent and the effect continues to remain a matter of trial and error every time the symphony is performed. Sledge-hammers, heavy mallets of all kinds have been tried, and what they are brought down upon

[1] *Gustav Mahler, Memories and Letters,* edited by Donald Mitchell (new enlarged edition), John Murray, London, 1973, p.99.

has ranged from great wooden blocks to the very orchestral platform itself.

pp.194/5   The giant chorale delivered by three each of trumpets and trombones in defiance of the first blow of fate is directed in the revised score to be played with the bells raised. The subsidiary 5th and 6th trumpets, on the other hand, are reduced in various ways, whether they are contributing harmonies or a counter-part, lest they obscure the clear lines of the other brass.

pp.196/8   One bar before 130 the great leaping trombone figure, which until here has been a leading voice, is reduced to a subsidiary role by being transferred to bassoons and bass clarinet. This also has the effect of allowing the cellos and basses (marked *sf* on each note) to be heard, as well as drawing the ear to the violins (strengthened now by the addition of the 2nds) and woodwind. All these answering phrases in dotted rhythm are made sharper and clearer, not only here but right to the end of the whole symphony, by the systematic substitution of dots by rests whenever this motif occurs, i.e. by changing

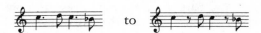

An extra pair of horns is added when they take over this figure at the second bar of **130**, thus making the violas and cellos redundant two bars later. Their new clean entry after the violins' swoop is far more vivid as a result and the swoop itself is joined by a third harp glissando. The bass drum is removed from the whole passage, as are further timpani strokes after the fifth bar of the page until **131**. Their effect had been to pin the music down too heavily and despite the pedal-point which remains on the deep sounding instruments, the overall effect should be one of soaring. The 1st violins now all play in unison at the upper octave instead of dividing, and the oboes, together with clarinets, are also raised an octave to join the violins and flutes as **131** is approached. Two bars before **131** the 2nd violins, relieved of their unnecessary unison with violas, make far more point of their sharp, short spread chords.

pp.198/201   At **131** itself the mood changes. Again the continuous percussion rolls of timpani and triangle proved too obtrusive and are abandoned after the two bars on p.198. (The missing dynamics in the piccolo are restored, bringing the instrument into line with flutes and violins.) The dots of the figure quoted above are again replaced by rests except in lower woodwind at the last bar of p.199, surely an oversight, though still to be found in Ratz. But most important, perhaps, is that the *schon langsamer* of **132** is anticipated by a *poco rit.* now appearing three bars before the end of p.199, and leading, moreover, to a new indication to the conductor, *Bereits 4/4* at **133**, signifying that the tempo is to be steadied so much more than Mahler had originally envisaged that the movement must be felt and beaten 'in 4' four bars earlier than he had prescribed in K1. A reduction in the number of horns and to the trumpets' dynamics (the latter substantially reduced) serves to accentuate the gentler mood and the woodwind are also cut back when they take over the melody from the violins.

pp.202/4   As a result of the more relaxed tempo in the preceding bars these stormy pages can now burst in at a quicker pulse without the risk of the conductor anticipating the cataclysm to come. The tempo here should in fact correspond with the *Allegro energico* of **110**, although there have been so many variations of pulse in the meantime that it is very easy to lose sight of this structural point.

In the second bar of p.203 the *fff* violins stop abruptly, leaving the upper woodwind to manage by themselves while the violins prepare for their next and more important entry. Their trills then continue in place of pizzicato on the first bar of the next page, an obviously logical as well as dramatic revision.

pp.205/7   This march forms the central episode of the movement, similar in some degree to the equally central march that is the kernel of the first movement of the Third Symphony, though this is immeasurably more sombre, even menacing in character. On p.215 the changes are confined to the omission of the bassoons for the space of two bars, and the dampening of the pulsations on horns and Rute (birch), the horns being reduced from eight to four and the Rute dropped from *ff* to *mf*. On p.206, however, these are left as they were, and the question must arise whether this was an oversight since at the second bar of the page a new diminuendo hairpin brings the lower strings down to a single *f* and the violas to an abrupt two-bar silence. Yet curiously the 2nd violins remain at an isolated *fff* and moreover the 1sts are even *added* for the brief motif

thus stressing it, perhaps in order to bring out its apparent similarity to one of the principal motifs of the first movement.

The bassoons no longer double the basses, but this is only the beginning of a fundamental re-thinking of these wind interjections. The simultaneous trombones' entry with the main *allegro* subject is cut out altogether while the cor anglais, clarinets and horn have their answering passage cut in half, not to obscure the strings' imitative entries. For these, while still of primary importance, are relieved from the previously overlong *ff*, being brought back to *f* though with a surge up to *sf* in the middle of the third bar of p.207, before once more dropping with a hairpin to the *mf* of the following bar. At the fourth bar of p.207 the basses are now sacrificed for three bars, in the last of which they are, however, replaced by the new rich colour of four unison bassoons. The reiterated notes on horns and Rute are removed altogether from the upper system of this page. At this point Ratz starts a wild goose chase.

In January 1907, the conductor Willem Mengelberg received a letter from Mahler in which the composer apologised for not being able to be present at a forthcoming performance of the Sixth Symphony, promising for his part to send the cowbells but asking Mengelberg to send him at once his (Mengelberg's) own full score as he wanted to put into it an important *retouche*.

When, after Mengelberg's death, the great conductor's score came to light, it was indeed found to contain such a *retouche* in the few bars after **136** and Ratz reasonably took it for granted that this was the passage Mahler was referring to in his letter. But Ratz also found a batch of *8ᵛᵃ* signs against the violins, viola and cello/bass parts in the first, second, third and fourth bars of p.207, and with far less reason decided that these were also part of the same *retouche* and must therefore be equally regarded as authentic and final. Moreover Redlich in Eul., whilst rightly berating Ratz for incorporating his deductions into the text instead of in a critical commentary where they belong, accepted his reasoning in respect of these questionable *8ᵛᵃ* signs, though failing to notice and account for the valid woodwind and horn revisions on p.209 which he thus unfortunately ignored. Consequently his remark in the Critical Commentary on p.xxxii of the Eulenburg Foreword also misrepresents the significance of the Mahler/Mengelberg correspondence.

As a matter of fact the *8ᵛᵃ* signs are highly doubtful for a number of reasons. In the first place Mahler in his letter clearly speaks of a single revision ('Ich möchte Ihnen eine sehr wichtige Retouche im letzten Satz hineinschreiben'), and the two passages in question are much too far apart to be regarded as a single *retouche*. Moreover, in his revision for K2 Mahler had already added appoggiatura chords to the violin parts at the beginning of the two bars before **135** and these would certainly have needed reconstituting. Mahler was the last person simply to push everything up an octave without regard to the attendant problems of detail. The violas also have a new appoggiatura-spread in the bar before **135** but this comes immediately after the proposed *loco*. The violins' *loco* comes only at **135** itself, while the cellos and basses are *loco* after only two bars (though the cellos jump up again for the last bar before **135**). The violas also have one isolated *loco* bar, three before **135**.

All this complicated to-ing and fro-ing plays havoc not only with the contrapuntal texture but with the lay-out of the string writing, and is from a variety of musical points of view unlikely and uncharacteristic to a degree. Furthermore, the woodwind entry at **135** would be overshadowed by so high a string passage as these bars would become whereas, on the contrary, the new figure needs to ride upon the previously established positioning of string tone. It would, to say the least, be very hard to prove that the 8va signs are in Mahler's own hand and the matter must remain a mystery.

In K2 the violins' chords of quadruple stopping at **135** are in a sudden and remarkable *p*. Horns and timpani are also reduced, though to *mf*, and the 1st violins' pizzicati in the second bar of **135** are removed altogether, thus avoiding an odd rhythmic conflict with the horns that can hardly have been intentional. The 2nd violins' doubling of the violas in this bar has also been taken out and the chords are accordingly more clearly featured. It is difficult to see why Mahler had originally given the 2nd violins fewer notes in their chords than the 1sts just in the last bar of p.207, but in K2 this discrepancy is removed and all the violins play the same.

pp.208/9   On p.208 the cor anglais and violins are struck out in bar 1; the *f* minims in horns 4 and 5 are reduced to a succession of *fp*'s (corresponding with the violas four bars later) and *ff* flutes double the plunging violins in the fourth bar. Yet strangely the bassoons no longer double the cellos and basses in their answering phrases which are, however, brought into line by starting an octave higher. Lest the horns and violins draw the attention away from the splendid imitation, they are carefully phrased with hairpins leading to a *p* three bars before **136**.

The cellos and basses still held Mahler's attention for a few more bars. The ascending and descending passage in the first two bars of the lower system of the page were plainly irresistible – any orchestral section would instinctively supply a rise and fall in dynamics. So Mahler prescribed the natural phrasing, following the passage with a rest for the basses. It is perhaps strange that he did not at the same time rest the cellos too – their *p* doubling of the violas' *f* (they too were *f* in K1) contributes little and robs them of freshness for their *ff* entry at **136**.

The next passage is not only greatly reduced both instrumentally and dynamically, but is the section cut down still further in Mengelberg's score and to which Mahler's letter might well be taken to refer although even here there can be no positive proof. However,

Ratz muddles the issue by restoring the K1 dynamic marks of the cellos in the second and third bars after **136** without comment of any kind. In K2 they, together with everyone else, are changed from *f* to *p* in these bars, although the cellos then have a new hairpin *crescendo* leading to *f* at the fourth bar, where the basses also join them. In the bar of **136** the clarinets and bassoons no longer double the accented minims of the violas which are now to be double-stopped.

Page 209 clearly caused Mahler much heart-searching. His first instinct had been to reduce dynamics whilst actually thickening the instrumental setting with additional wind-doublings. Also the 2nd violins double the 1sts a bar later than in K1, thus now contributing to a newly orchestrated crescendo from *p* to *ff*. But the Mengelberg score once more takes out all the added wind (oboes, clarinets and horns) together with the doubling 2nd violins. The trombones on the other hand show a precisely opposite revision. Their entry had been marked back in K2 from *ff sempre* to *p*, with a gradual swell though to no more than a single *f*. Moreover, bearing in mind his new general drop in dynamics, Mahler had in K2 taken out the 2nd trombone but Ratz puts it back again as in K1, presumably on the basis of Mengelberg's score, though he does not say so.

Certainly the effect of this latest revision is to create a far more gradual crescendo of the figure:

and to make more point of the curious reversal of dynamics in K2, whereby the violins are marked back to *p* while the horns, who are playing the figure itself, are raised to *f*. For contrast of colour the background minims are taken away from a further group of horns and given to woodwind.

pp.210/15   In the second bar of p.210 the four-horn unison line was originally intended as a powerful imitation. In the event it must have proved too startling, for Mahler weakened it by making the horns play in thirds, with markedly less brash effect.

At **137** the timpani is suppressed altogether and no longer reappears until the entry at **139**, which is undoubtedly more dramatic in consequence.

Mahler originally instructed that the pressing forward of the music at this point should be imperceptible, but in K2 removed this (bracketed) reservation. The music must now really surge straightaway, without delaying until the *Noch etwas drängender* on the following page.

From four bars before **138** to **139** it was the horn and trumpet parts that came under scrutiny. First and foremost Mahler varied the dynamics of the four leading horns in the bars preceding **138**, making a far more interesting feature of their descending phrase than the relentless *sempre ff* of K1 had suggested. Then the rising figure both at **138** itself and four bars later is taken away from the 1st trumpet to enable him to enter in the following bars with a clean and striking effect. The brass are now unmuted, including the eight horns, except only for the 4th to 6th trumpets whose role is also severely curtailed.

On pp.214 to 215 Mahler took the opportunity of substituting an *immer 4/4* after the *allmählich beruhigend* on p.214 for the misleading 4/4 on p.215. (The missing [D] sharp in the 3rd horn at the fifth bar of p.215 escaped Mahler's notice as it did also both Ratz and Redlich.)

pp.216/17   Figure **140** marks the second hammer blow and the beginning of the third and shortest section of this vast development. This time the hammer was at first reinforced not only by timpani but by bass drum, cymbals and a prolonged tam-tam stroke as well. Yet whereas at **127** Mahler had added the bass drum to the first hammer blow in K2, here at **140** he realised that he had overdone it and added a footnote to the effect that the cymbals and tam-tam were only there in case the hammer would not by itself be overwhelming. But the bass drum was not included in the footnote and hence becomes again a positive adjunct to the second hammer blow which, from the phrasing of the footnote, is clearly intended to be even more overwhelming than the first. Unfortunately, however, this cuts across Alma Mahler's account of the first performance in her Memoirs:

We looked in for a moment at the supper-party after the concert for the sake of appearances. Mahler was in such a state that I dared not let him go alone; but his gloom vanished when he got there. He introduced Mengelberg to me; he seemed to me like Loge. I was planted ceremoniously next to Strauss at supper. 'Why ever does Mahler smother his effect in the last movement?' he said. 'He gets his fortissimo and then damps it down. Can't understand that at all.' He never did understand. He spoke simply as the showman. Anyone who understands the symphony at all understands why the first blow is the strongest, the second weaker and the third – the death blow – the weakest of all. Perhaps the momentary effect might be greater in the inverse order. But that is not the point.[1]

Alma was not actually quite right here but it is perhaps understandable that she had bridled at Strauss's tactless comment. Yet in point of fact he had put his finger on a salient point of orchestration, supreme professional as he was above all: Mahler also quickly came to appreciate that the more one tries to reinforce the hammer blows with other percussion effects the more one actually counteracts rather than strengthens the peculiar ferocity of their impact.

The whirlwind that follows the second hammer blow is intensified in K2 by a mass of upper woodwind during the third, fourth and fifth bars of p.216 as well as by the reintroduction of cellos over two bars, five and six after **140**.

As at **129**, the brass are here marked to play 'bells up' in the revision, as are the muted second trio of trumpets at **141**. On the other hand, the leading trumpets drop their sound unexpectedly with a new *ffp* three bars before **141**, perhaps to lend greater emphasis to the giant leap of the trombone and tuba, but also to prepare for the outburst of the woodwind in the following bar.

pp.218/21 The revision of these last four pages of the development largely concentrates on the correction of details. Countless rests are substituted for dots in the figure quoted on p.134 above, which is extensively worked out in these pages. Accents and sforzandi are added in places where their previous omissions now appear as over-

[1] Ibid., p.100.

sights; the trumpet chord at **142** is cut short, leaving only the 6th player to enter *p* ——— and so lead to the *f* solo line in which the 5th trumpet rejoins him. In the last bar of p.221 a *ff* timpani is added to the savage *sf* chords which usher in the reprise.

pp.222/4   As at the opening of the Finale, the celesta needed amplification, but this time it is done in a different way – i.e. by using more and quicker notes so that the arpeggio ends an octave higher. Both hands are again instructed to be used but one after the other instead of together.

The string tremolos are strengthened by raising the cellos an octave to play in unison with the others for two bars. They then rest briefly to remove their mutes, before re-entering at their original pitch in the third bar of p.223. This is in order that the great unison string *ff* should be wholly unmuted, for which purpose provision had also to be made for the unmuting of the violas by redistributing some more of the tremolos.

As on p.150 the harp glissando now lasts three beats, and the unmuted brass with the motto major triad drop quickly to *pp*, to allow the muted players to come through more clearly as they crescendo towards the fatal minor tonality that succeeds it. (The missing *ff* in the muted horns at the beginning of p.224 is restored, but the *p* in the unmuted horns and trumpets should already have been suppressed in K2. In K1 it had marked the end of a decrescendo from *ff*, but now the hairpin begins its descent from *pp*.)

The timpani are made more sharply dramatic by changing to wooden sticks seven bars before **144**, whereas the side drum is on the contrary abruptly reduced in dynamics after its initial *ff*. Commas are added to the cello/bass semibreves two bars before **144** as in the corresponding place before **104**, though with the further addition of repeated down-bows.

pp.224/5   At **144** the missing *arco* is restored to cellos (as also to basses seven bars later) and the now necessary *mit Dämpfer* added. Curiously the corresponding indication for 2nd violins and violas is already present although redundant in K1. The delaying of the bells' entry by one bar brings this return into line with the parallel entry on p.152. One wonders whether K1 constituted a misprint or a variation of which Mahler on reflection thought better. A curious point is that in the earlier passage the bells are notated:

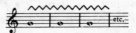

whereas here they appear a note lower:

this difference surviving in K2 and Ratz. Whether Mahler had meant some difference in intonation (bearing in mind that the bells are of indefinite pitch) must remain a matter of conjecture.

pp.226/8   The revisions here are more ruthless than those corresponding on p.152. Where previously the wood-wind supporting the strings, harps and celesta had been reduced to **ppp**, here – the phrase being extended – not only are the clarinets again so marked but the flute, cor anglais and bassoon (who had continued the figure) are all cut right out, excepting only two bars of a single **ppp** flute that accordingly becomes more meaningful. Four bars of background 2nd violin notes are also sacrificed. On the other hand the 4th horn solo (corresponding with the solo for the same player on p.152) is not only marked up as before but additionally doubled by the 2nd horn. Again, where the basses have ceased to support the contra during the last two bars of p.226, a tuba now takes over the pedal F, a very rumbly note, however much Mahler may mark it **pp**. It is perhaps strange that the tuba is not now allowed to continue its support for the one further bar on the next page. More-over, there is an air of incompleteness about the beginning of p.227, with the missing trombone rests in the first two bars that remain unnoticed in K2 and Ratz.

As on p.183 (of which this is equally a reprise), the trumpet and trombone are now muted and it is interest-ing to note that Mahler no longer considered it necessary to advocate the use of the alto trombone (as suggested in K1) for this fairly high and exposed solo. Perhaps he found that players handled it on the tenor more easily than he had expected.

The harps now play chords instead of single notes during the two bars before **146**, and the celesta part is filled out and its passage extended so that it plays every crotchet for six whole bars from its entry at the second last bar of p.227. The cellos are also unmuted at **146** – perhaps this was an omission, as in K1 there is no indication here or later where they should remove their mutes. The harps now crescendo to *f* as **147** is approached and the tremolando cellos are further reinforced in the last two bars by violas, who have abandoned the whole of their pizzicato passage for the purpose; the increase in harp tone more than compensates for this loss. At **146** the high clarinet solo is doubled in revision and further joined by the D clarinet followed by flute. Mahler was nothing if not courageous.

An important change now begins in the tempo scheme. In place of the *Etwas fliessender* (*aber immer 4/4*) Mahler simply gives *Stets 4/4*. This might seem redundant unless one notices that at the parallel place after **121** the conductor is specifically instructed to beat minims and so might be led to do so again here. (Unfortunately K2 only changed the marking at the head of the page, so that both old and new are present simultaneously; but Ratz rectifies this error.) Indeed, unlike the earlier context, the whole transition is to be made with a far more gradual stepping up of the tempo.

pp.228/9   Thus the adoption of a quieter pulse at **147** is also removed and the displaced second subject appears at a steadier tempo than in the corresponding passage at **117**. The change of mood is now dependent on the complete change of instrumentation and on the *Grazioso* marking. This is hard to bring off convincingly and the revisions suggest that Mahler himself may have experienced some difficulty in achieving it satisfactorily. There are even signs that at some point in the sketches a cut was made here, and this might be endorsed by the curious change in the oboe's designation. Here and here alone in the entire symphony Mahler drops the old-fashioned H for Hoboe and uses the modern German Oboe (thereby encouraging Ratz, instead of bringing this exception into line, to change every other one of the 250-odd pages). This oboe who bridges the join at **147** can easily sound rather gauche and Mahler therefore adds the indication *leggiero*, which is also given to the repeat of the phrase on the solo violin eight bars later.

At **148** Mahler specifically instructs the solo violin to play with the tutti in case the rests in his individual stave prove misleading. One wishes that many a composer might have profited by this example. It is a curious custom to mark rests when such a solo line is no longer independent, irrespective of the assumption that the player will take over the leadership of the section as soon as it is practicable.

The 2nd cellos are given their missing *arco* at **148** in K2 and in the following bar one of Mahler's most typical and graphic injunctions, 'Ton!', is added. It is not difficult to understand his purpose here: where the lower line is in unison with basses it is convenient to divide the section into blocks of front and rear desks, in which case the back desks need encouragement. Mahler then takes the opportunity to heighten the expression marks not only for these players but also for basses and bassoon four bars after **148**.

Four bars before the end of p.229, the change to *mf* solely in the 2nd violins emphasizes the contrast of dynamics with the 1sts, whose entirely different marking was previously confined to the last two bars of the page. This is another characteristically imaginative use of orchestral colour, and one that Mahler exploited throughout his life. It takes for granted his platform formation with the 1st and 2nd violins to the left and right respectively, for with all the violins bunched together on one side the effect of such opposed dynamics makes no impression whatever.

pp.230/3   Page 230 is one of the few pages left entirely unaltered. It is interesting to compare this peroration of the premature second subject with that of the corresponding subject of the first movement (Alma's theme) reproduced on p.86. This time, however, there is a violent interruption and in K2 Mahler accentuates the incompleteness of the statement with commas at **150** on p.231, marked all the way down the page.

In the next hectic section Mahler had some important second thoughts. The woodwind *ff* doubling of the violins was too strident and eight horns too many. At the *più mosso*, however, the oboes and clarinets are brought into prominence and are instructed to play with raised bells. To get a more startling entry Mahler even sacrificed their up-beat swoop. The violins whom they reinforce in this piercing way are marked up from *sf* to no less than *fff*.

The instruction to the 4th flute to take piccolo is only a precautionary measure; already in K1 there are two piccolos on p.234, but one suspects that the lack of specific directive led to error in the part and irritating loss of time in rehearsal. The new and unusual rehearsal figure **150½** at the second bar of p.233 also reflects the frustration suffered by the composer when trying frenetically to get the passage to his satisfaction.

pp.233/5   It is not surprising, therefore, to find a great many changes over the next few pages. It is a feverish passage and Mahler struggled with himself as much as with his sorely-tried players in his determination to put his finger on what was wrong. Those eight *ff* unison horns in just the second bar of **150½** were attracting too much attention at the expense of the other lines. Four were ample, and the 2nd horn quartet could continue its harmonic function supported moreover by a tremolo on the violas, whereas the 2nd violins can now reinforce the upper horn line. The trombones' harsh tone colour was also too much of a shock in this context: their chord must go altogether. The 1st trumpet solo must make much more of a crescendo – up to a true *f* at the quavers of his counter-phrase. (K2 makes a confusing error here in forgetting to strike out the listing of 'Tr.2' at the beginning of p.233, but Ratz puts this right.)

The revision of the basses and contra in the last bar but one of the page raises an important issue. In K1 the basses suddenly switch to the upper octave, producing what might technically be regarded as a true unison with the cellos. On the other hand the normally notated unison – the basses sounding an octave lower – is in fact far stronger as well as a more natural unison, which Mahler restored in this bar, applying the same logic to the contrabassoon. This was a lesson which Schönberg and many of his followers, writing their scores at concert pitch, might well have taken to heart.

In the last bar of the page the timpani's entry is drastically shortened, first dropped to *p* and then disappearing altogether in order to leave the stage clear for the 2nd timpani's brutal hammering of the march motif. The omission of the cymbals also increases the menace of that pounding low E. The screaming top phrases are rendered even shriller with all the flutes – two playing piccolo – now joining in a wild unison at the beginning of p.234, followed by four each of oboes and clarinets in the figures three bars and one bar before **151**. For greater incisiveness the violins' tremolo stops on the short notes of the phrases in these bars.

Attention is next focussed on the horns, who have a pair of truly Wagnerian doom-laden cadences each now marked with a diminuendo from *fff* to *p*. Then starting *p* at **151**, they crescendo steadily and menacingly from accented semibreve to accented semibreve, reaching *f* – but significantly no more – by the end of p.235. At the same time Mahler realised that the cellos and basses need no brigade of bassoons plus bass clarinet to double their vehement ascending passage; they have more cutting edge on their own.

pp.236/8   These pages in K2 look quite stark when compared with the original scoring, as so much superfluous detail has been thrown out. On p.236 especially, there had been a great deal of arpeggiando to-ing and fro-ing of which now nothing remains in the wind and less than half in the strings, mostly replaced by gaunt semibreves. There is some loss of imaginative colouristic scoring to be regretted but the greater power of bold lines was the main concern in this last and greatest build-up in the whole mighty scheme.

As in the first movement, the percussion is vastly reduced, giving – as is the way with percussion – far more drama to what remains, whether the triangle's jangle in the bar before **152** (itself the survivor of two such entries, and further brought down in a hairpin from its initial *ff*), or the hammer-like low E's of the 2nd timpani, now featured through the suppression of the originally relentless rolling of the other timpanist.

A splendid new dramatic feature is introduced in K2 whereby the 1st and 2nd horns enter on a low B two bars before **152** and then execute a leap of nearly two octaves to their high G of the next bar. They then continue their upward sweep to take over the main theme in unison with the massed upper woodwind, in which they are joined, moreover, not by one, but two more horns, the 5th and 7th. These four horns now continue this passionate unison for the remainder of the page, undisturbed by other horns playing chords or moving parts. All have been removed, as have the trumpet chords which in alternation with the other six horns had previously blazed out *fortissimo* chords of their own. This whole effect has been erased in order to achieve the maximum dramatic simplicity. The harmonic background now rests therefore entirely with 2nd violins and violas scrubbing out a tremolo as hard as they can go. The upward flashing scales are left to the 1st violins alone and, punctuated as they are by bar-long rests, are easily accomplished with all the brilliance that can be desired.

The lower strings, deprived of horn support – the horns are now all silent during the last four bars before **153** – are given a further *ff* by way of reminder, and the crescendi of the trumpets are carefully graded where previously Mahler had given them *crescendo* after *crescendo* following upon earlier marks of already no less than *ff*.

pp.238/41 Fig.**153** represents a key moment in the structure of the reprise and is therefore a powerful climax, but even so it cannot afford to be too arresting. It is still only a milestone on the road, and Mahler realised that he had made of it virtually an end in itself, by the time he had broadened the tempo and hammered out every stress in the motifs with cymbals and two timpanists each addressing a pair of drums with unabating emphasis. There was a serious danger of stealing the thunder of the real hammer whose third death-blow should provide the ultimate climactic *coup de grâce*. All this percussion is struck out, therefore, as are also many reinforcements of the main motif in the lower instruments. The trumpets and trombones are replaced by horns and clarinets (the bass clarinet, of all instruments, is marked to play with its bell raised) and even the bass trombone and tuba, who remain, are reduced in dynamics. The motif of the lower strings is brought into prominence by taking out the tremolos and substituting trills played with repeated down-bows.

The *Molto pesante – Tempo sehr anhaltend* is taken away altogether and in its place the *Tempo I (Allegro energico)* 4/4 is brought forward from the third bar of p.239 (as in K1) to stand at **153**. Here at last is the beginning of the delayed Primary Section of the Recapitulation and this needs to be emphasized by a return, as abrupt as may be, to the tempo and character of **110**, especially in view of the motivic overlap in the upper strings and woodwind.

Some confusion is presented by the trumpet mutings as they still stand even in Ratz. The *Dämpfer ab* in 3rd trumpet no longer applies since he now plays the bar before **153** unmuted. The same applies to the *offen* on p.239, whereas the *offen* prescribed for trumpets 4, 5 and 6 is in contradiction to K1 in which they played this passage muted (together with another now deleted). These marks should all be removed from the later scores as unnecessary and confusing.

Mahler recognized that the exultant trumpet passage rising to the top C sharp is essentially a balancing after-phrase of the overlapping second subject and must not, as the result of the tempo change, be made to sound like a primary statement. Moreover **154**, being the beginning of another answering period, must also not be over-emphasized. The bar before **154**, however, is an essential link-bar and can be vulgarly dramatized as such marches commonly are – hence the extra spotlighting of the descending scale with bass trombone and tuba in unison (cf. the corresponding bar of Elgar's *Cockaigne* Overture with its trombone glissandi).

Trumpets and side drums have hairpins down instead of up (horns all come down from their *fff*) and the tremolando 2nd violins and violas are given a most subtle change. In K1 the quaver with which they end is tied back:

a nicety of phrasing implying that the last note should be phrased away, rather than actually tied without re-sounding. In the revision the ties have been removed and this can only mean that particular care need no longer be taken to avoid a bump.

At **154** the bass trombone, having been otherwise occupied as we have seen, no longer even attempts to double the fanfare of the 3rd player. One timpani, though marked *ff*, replaces two marked *f*, a careful distinction, and the trumpets no longer double the upper strings' continuation of the march-theme, this becoming a far more interesting variation of colour in what is essentially a tutti peroration. *A propos* the theme itself, experience had taught Mahler that a low end-note of a phrase often tends to sound weak and he therefore takes elaborate steps to make good any conceivable deficiencies of the final D with the reinforcement of cellos (for them an evocative high note), as well as oboes (in their case a penetrating and reedy low note) and by making all the players sustain over into the third beat.

In the third bar of **154** pizzicato violins savagely pick out the edges of the shrill woodwind trills, and the top of this phrase is emphasized not only by upper strings (the violas *arco* instead of *pizz*.) but also by two trumpets in unison at the top of their compass and marked *p* – a very interesting and courageous touch. The violas no longer double the semiquaver rising up-beat figures of the violins; lying so high they must have merely added splash rather than the vehemence Mahler had envisaged. The timpani have also lost their two quavers in the second bar, though the *fortissimo* crotchets two bars later are certainly still present and the more startling for the previous omission. In the second last bar of p.241, *ff* violas are added to the lower pizzicato notes of the violins. This apparently insignificant addition makes an extraordinary difference to the effect of these biting interjections. On the last crotchet of the page the cymbals are sacrificed: they must have completely swamped the glockenspiel and triangle.

pp.242/5   The adding of two down-bows for the pair of minims, now a salient feature of the principal theme of the *Allegro energico,* had first been instigated at **110** and here recurs many times, throughout the string department between **153** and **156**.

At the sixth bar of p.243 the glitter of the glockenspiel is added to the spiky violin and woodwind passage. This corresponds with its use during the previous two pages and certainly adds point to what had been a very isolated reappearance in the single bar five after **156**.

The harp glissando at the beginning of p.243 is, like so many of the harp glissandi of this movement, started a beat earlier so as to have more time to make its effect. This ushers in the trumpets' major-minor Fate motto which is once again given to entirely unmuted brass.

The frenzied violins are twice dropped to *mf* and deprived of their supporting violas between **156** and **157**, with the purpose of exposing the all-important extended trumpet solo, though the change also adds far greater interest to their own part than if they are playing away incessantly for dear life. The massed oboes' doublings, whether of just three notes of the trumpet or later of the violins, are also cut out, perhaps surprisingly. Mahler may have felt that he was using too many mixed colours in this essentially tutti symphony.

One bar of the timpani passage on p.244 has gone, thus making more point of its rhythmic emphasizing of the horns' second bar. Two bars before **157** the 1st violins hand over their passage-work to the violas, to prepare for a new impetus at the rising scale. The 2nds, however, still play everything. To make sure that nothing prevents this flamboyant gesture coming right through, the second trio of trumpets are removed from the crescendo into **157**; and to ensure further that the similarity of their tone does not cause confusion with the chromatic wail of the 1st and 2nd trumpets, they put their mutes on again – though only for four bars. In this section they spend as much time putting on and taking off their mutes as they do in playing. Yet it is not unjustified fussiness: the use here of two muted trumpets in the third bar of **157** to double the open 3rd trumpet, who crescendos while they fade away, is a remarkable piece of imaginative orchestration.

A very curious revision occurs at the third bar of **157**: the violas actually stop in the most unnatural way, leaving the woodwind and trumpet to continue the line between them in alternation. This has the effect of lightening the central texture which is now thrown to and fro with a brilliance and sharpness of timbre it had never acquired when forming part of a continuous multichrome counterpoint.

pp.246/7

In the bar before **158** there is another extended harp glissando – this time given three whole beats in which to herald a still stronger and more menacing return of the Fate motifs.

On p.247 Mahler felt with reason that he had made ample use of the solo trumpet and from the third bar of the page removed it in favour of the oboes and clarinets. These had admittedly been playing already in K1 but they are now marked to play with their bells up, and if the musicians can be persuaded to do this wholeheartedly it can be found to produce not merely an increase in dynamic but a totally different tone-quality. There is, however, a disconcerting tendency amongst players to regard the demand as extravagant nonsense to be good-humouredly guyed at rehearsal and discreetly overlooked at performance.

p.248

Four bars before **159** the flutes had doubled the muted 5th and 6th trumpets but they are removed in the revision. Certainly it made little effect other than softening the edgy quality of the trumpets, and the clean new start at **159** together with the oboes and clarinets has much to commend it. These latter instruments have extra accentuated semibreves at the third bar of the page, to correspond with the semibreves two bars earlier which now alternate with cor anglais and bassoons, though in a *p* that contrasts with the *ff* of the others. This has the additional purpose of emphasizing the notes with which the violins start their leaping motif.

pp.249/53

The woodwind doublings of the wild violin passage-work on pp.249/50 is greatly reduced in K2. Only the clarinets now double the 2nd violins and violas as they take over from the 1sts at the beginning of p.250. The flutes and D clarinets enter together with the 1st violins for the upward rush, the oboes only at **160** itself. An *etwas drängend* is added to p.250, so feverish has the excitement become, though the conductor has still to keep firm control over himself as well as his forces. This is a truly enormous span and even though by **161** on p.252 an *alla breve* is reached there is a precautionary *aber nicht eilen!* that must not be overlooked.

The new fleetness of the *etwas drängend* carries with it a mobility of texture which percussion, whether purely colouristic like triangle and cymbal rolls or rhythmic as with drum beats, tends to counteract. So Mahler wipes the percussion slate practically clean, leaving none at all on pp.250/1, on p.252 a couple of isolated but well placed timpani strokes, and the one tremendous cymbal clash that is still directed to be played with 'several cymbals' – that is to say, as many pairs as players can be mustered to play them.

The removal of the elaborate timpani part on p.251 constitutes an important creative re-thinking, for so striking would it have been that without it the remaining lines attract infinitely more attention; hence especially the heightened expectancy of these bars as they drive headlong into the coarse ('roh') *fff* of the eight horns at the beginning of p.252. This was to have been reinforced at the end of the bar by the four trombones, but so over-powering must have been the impact even in their original single *f* that Mahler decided to reserve them for their entry two bars later, in logical succession to the trumpets. The original trombone chordal entry is now diverted to lower woodwind and strings, the latter marked *wild* and in the new avoidance of brass doublings the glory of each group is clearly and separately differentiated. Mahler, taking a leaf out of Berlioz's book, (cf. the *Marche au Supplice* fig.58) here gives a footnote stressing that the dissonant trumpet C, sounding F, is correct.

Mahler next discovered that the 1st and 2nd violins' unison trills, set against the bevy of woodwind also trilling, would have less cumulative power than if they did something different from one another. So at the third bar of p.253 the 1st violins change to tremolo until the wind are launched on their headlong semiquavers.

Four bars before **161** the jettisoning of the eight horns plus two trumpets had resulted in the loss of an essential harmony note. So four horns are reinstated, purely to supply the missing F sharp which supports the trombones' rising phrase.

The descending swoop into **161** is simplified and the harps' glissando given not more beats this time, but an extra octave that makes the effect twice as powerful.

pp.253/5   Daring as it was to entrust the last descending imitation just to very low horns and trumpets in the bar before **161**, it enabled Mahler to start the spiritually uplifting *alla breve* with a stark boldness all too necessary after the previous cataclysm. Mahler's hero has fought free of the terrible elements that had threatened to engulf him. In this dawning of victory there is a *religioso* quality that needs the utmost clarity of contrapuntal style, and Mahler's revisions are all made with the aim of avoiding as far as possible the premature use of instruments sooner or later earmarked for salient imitative entries. Thus the violins are now held back not only in the first bars of **161** but also for the whole of p.254, in preparation for their fine entry with the leaping phrase at the beginning of p.255, in which they are joined by all four flutes whose role is changed for the purpose. The violas make their first entry already in the third bar of **161** (though also after a new period of rest), but when after a four-bar respite they burst in together with the wind they now drop out again after only a single bar instead of joining forces with the succeeding violin imitation. For it is their own line at **162** that must be well prepared, approaching the unison with basses and bassoon with an octave leap from the opposite direction. This now enters, purposefully leading the way for the rich descending chord-leaps in the succeeding bars.

Similar newly-exposed entries can be found in the wind – the trombones in the last bar of p.253, the band of unison clarinets in the following bar for whose benefit the trombones' dynamic is vastly reduced, the lower four horns four bars before **162**, all are clarified by anticipatory rests.

At the same time, there has been some judicious thinning of unnecessary doublings within individual instrumental groups themselves – one trumpet each instead of two for the *ff* entries in the seventh and ninth bars of p.254; two trombones instead of three, and four horns instead of eight, six bars before **162**; indeed only two horns instead of eight, two bars before **162**. The lead-in to the second contrapuntal outburst of this Brucknerian figure is magically slender, despite the vehemence of the united 1st and 2nd violins.

pp.256/9

The cadential phrase of the second and third bars of p.256 is lightened by the removal of the 3rd trumpet (the 6th player now playing alone), of the violas' tremolando thickening of the 4th and 5th trumpets' chromatic phrase, and of four of the eight horns. The latter in particular are being saved for their majestic utterance of what might be thought of as a song of victory which they and the cellos (who previously had a quite purposeless sustained line) have taken over from the trombones. The change is a psychological one, for the horns and cellos have greater warmth and breadth for this noble paean. Moreover, the trombones of K1 had been pitted against a battery of percussion. Here again is a programmatic change, the background threat of the martial Fate-rhythm having been over-emphasized at this moment of apparent triumph. Thus all that remains of the thunderous pair of timpanists reinforced by side drums, cymbals and triangle, is a single timpani together with pizzicato double basses. Curiously one solitary bar of the original percussion parts appears at the beginning of p.257 and can still be seen in Ratz though it is inconceivable that Mahler meant it to survive.

On p.257 the *Beruhigend* is more carefully graded in the trumpets' decrescendo from the new *ff* of the 1st and 2nd players to the finer *pp* of the 5th left now undoubled by the 6th player. And the final song of momentary exultancy at **163** is made the more poignant by beginning the long crescendo from a universal *p* or *pp* (the upper 1st violin E is an exception that seems to have slipped through the net – Mahler may or may not have meant this) and by holding the tempo back in a general marking of *pesante*.

The coda brings the return of catastrophe. Just as each of the main sections of the movement had begun with the very opening bars of the whole Finale, so does this final scene of the drama. Each time there were variations of detail, but the main elements were always present. The omission of the celesta in K1 was therefore in all likelihood an oversight that is duly rectified by a sharp ringing chord on the second half of the bar of **164**, corresponding in miniature to the violent splash of harps and pizzicato violins that had marked the first bar of the development section at **120**. At that point the celesta had only been used as an auxiliary colour together with the string tremolos. Here it once more has a primary function.

pp.260/1   Once again the harp glissando is extended, this time from one to three beats. The last beat was also originally reinforced by a run-up on flutes and oboes, but the oboes are replaced by the celesta, a strange choice and without precedent in this context.

The climax of this swoop is the third hammer blow which, in Mahler's own words, 'fells the hero like a tree'. It comes together with the Fate mottos – the major-minor triads on the brass and the pounding rhythms on percussion but, despite the significance this gives it, the actual instrumental setting is perceptibly less over-powering than its predecessors and does therefore bear out both Strauss's criticism and to some degree Alma Mahler's retort quoted above (p.136).

However, as has been discussed earlier, Mahler became intensely and superstitiously afraid of a certain self-identification with his own hero. At the first performance he was utterly beside himself with terror. Alma describes the scene with quite hilarious vividness:

> None of his works moved him so deeply at its first hearing as this. We came to the last rehearsals, to the dress-rehearsal – to the last movement with its three great blows of fate. When it was over, Mahler walked up and down in the artists' room, sobbing, wringing his hands, unable to control himself. Fried, Gabrilovitch, Buths and I stood transfixed, not daring to look at one another. Suddenly Strauss came noisily in, noticing nothing. 'Mahler, I say, you've got to conduct some funeral overture or other tomorrow before the Sixth – their mayor has died on them. So vulgar, that sort of thing – But what's the matter? What's up with you? But –' and out he went as noisily as he had come in, quite unmoved, leaving us petrified.[1]

Before long, Mahler became unable to conduct that dreaded third hammer blow; and ultimately he had no option but to suppress it utterly from the actual score.

Accordingly K2 presents a greatly watered down version of this moment, with side drum and timpani

[1] Ibid., p.100.

both muted, the trombones replaced by bassoons (!), the muted trumpets softened by clarinets, even the strings weakened by a diminuendo on their second bar as well as by the removal of the lower cellos and bass lines, and the striking out altogether of the last stabbing wood-wind minor triad two bars before **165**. This version is, of course, reproduced by Ratz and is also included in a facsimile of the relevant page of K2 by Redlich as p.xxxi of his Eulenburg Foreword.

Redlich states that by 1910 Mahler had seriously begun to contemplate the reinstating of the third hammer blow but unfortunately we have no positive evidence of this. Nevertheless, there no longer remains any moral obligation to omit the third blow or to observe the attendant revisions which robbed this moment of its drama in deference to the last score published in Mahler's lifetime. Fate cannot still be felt to stand threateningly over the composer who has been dead and beyond her menace, real or imaginary, for over sixty years. Superstition must play no further part in what is now primarily an artistic decision. Only the meaning and structure of the work can offer guidance in such an ethical problem. Mahler's intentions were clear enough and the three hammer blows should be restored. Conceivably the only valid way to play the symphony with only two hammer blows would be to make absolutely sure that *everyone* witnessing the performance is fully aware that there were supposed to be three strokes but that for personal reasons the composer had suppressed the last, the Death Blow. Perhaps the percussionist might then raise the hammer before the crucial moment but on a sign from the conductor lay it down again, though this is of course a melodramatic and non-musical solution more suitable for a television feature programme than a symphony concert.

pp.261/3   The whole of the concluding dirge is built on the dotted figure which in K2 is systematically changed bar by bar, with rests substituted for dots, whether a quaver or a crotchet in value. The sustained background chord of D major turning to minor is now robbed of some extra poignancy supplied in K1 by a C clarinet (the D clarinet player had changed for specifically this one purpose), doubled at the octave by the cor anglais. This is not to say, however, that the meaningful F sharp which drops to F natural is now absent, for it is still part of the lower woodwind-chord in the other clarinets and the bassoons. A *ritenuto* is added at the third bar of p.262, justifying, and leading towards, the *immer langsamer* of **166**.

Even the close of the symphony with its harsh intrusion of the Fate rhythm, this time truly *ff* with no holds barred, is slightly revised, the trumpets and side drum tailing away earlier than Mahler had at first envisaged, and separated by a comma from the final string *p* pizzicato with which the gigantic symphony ends. This sudden explosion presents a final image of the implacable figure of Fate as the chief protagonist in the work, a conception taken over by Elgar with striking success in the closing bars of his symphonic study *Falstaff,* where the stern theme of the young king Henry V is also thrown curtly across the canvas with a terrifying element of shock after a funeral *pp* fades out, also to be followed by a separate and final soft pizzicato unison. The influence of Mahler was to be far-reaching but nowhere so widely or so universally as in this great symphony.